Walk the Wessex Ridgeway
in Dorset

THE WYVERN

Originally all scaly creatures with bat-like wings were 'dragons'. These were often depicted as serpents, without legs, or sometimes with just two. With the arrival in the late medieval bestiaries of a four-footed version, a distinction came to be made between the wyvern (with two legs) and the dragon (with four). The dragon probably entered British armoury as the standard of the Roman cohort and remained in the symbolism of the post-Roman era and in the 'burning-dragon' of Cadwalleder from which the red dragon of Wales is derived. It is also associated with the ancient kingdom of Wessex and a golden wyvern appears in the Bayeux Tapestry as Harold's personal device. It is therefore an eminently suitable emblem for the Wessex Ridgeway and we hope to see it adopted as such if the route ever receives official recognition.

Walk the Wessex Ridgeway
in Dorset

A guide to the Dorset section of this new long-distance path,
with eleven circular walks

Priscilla Houstoun

dpc
Dorset Publishing Company
in association with
The Ramblers' Association
Dorset Area

This edition first published 1994 by
Wincanton Press
National School, North Street, Wincanton, Somerset BA9 9AT

Previous edition published by
The Ramblers' Association - Dorset Area
First edition September 1988
Second impression January 1989

Royalties to Ramblers' Association - Dorset Area

Text design by Mentor DTP, Bruton, Somerset

While every attempt has been made to provide accurate descriptions and maps,
the author and publishers cannot be held responsible for changes that
take place after the publication of this book.

Distributed by Dorset Publishing Company from the Wincanton Press
National School, North Street, Wincanton, Somerset BA9 9AT.
Telephone: 0963 32583 until 1995, then 01963 32583

ISBN 0 948699 37 X

CONTENTS

PREFACE

The Wessex Ridgeway is a new route, worked out by members of the Ramblers' Association Areas of Wilts and Dorset during the Eighties. It was designed to link the Ridgeway LDP from Avebury to the Dorset coast at Lyme Regis and to follow a line along which at least some stretches of the ancient track, the Great Ridgeway, is believed to have run. The route is not yet an official National Trail and is consequently not waymarked as such. However, the two County Councils involved, Wilts and Dorset, have agreed to adopt the Wessex Wyvern as the route symbol and waymarking the Dorset section is under way.

The Ramblers' Association has published an official Guide to the whole route (see book list at back) and this local Guide has been written for walkers holidaying in Dorset who want to enjoy parts of the route and some of the countryside around it. It is our hope that, having sampled our share of it, they will arm themselves with the official Guide and walk the whole route.

The circular walks described in the second half of this book are all based on the main route. They can either be started from it, or from suitable spots where cars can be left. In each case, the appropriate Pathfinder and Landranger maps are noted.

The author would like to thank:

Brian Pantion for arranging the typing of her manuscripts and for "professionalising" her hand-drawn maps,

Laurence Main who supplied lavish information about the Armada beacons,

Stephen Friar who did the research on the Wessex Wyvern and Andrew Jamieson who drew it, and

The County Surveyor's Rights of Way staff for their encouragement and help in planning the route and for dealing with defects almost within minutes of their being reported.

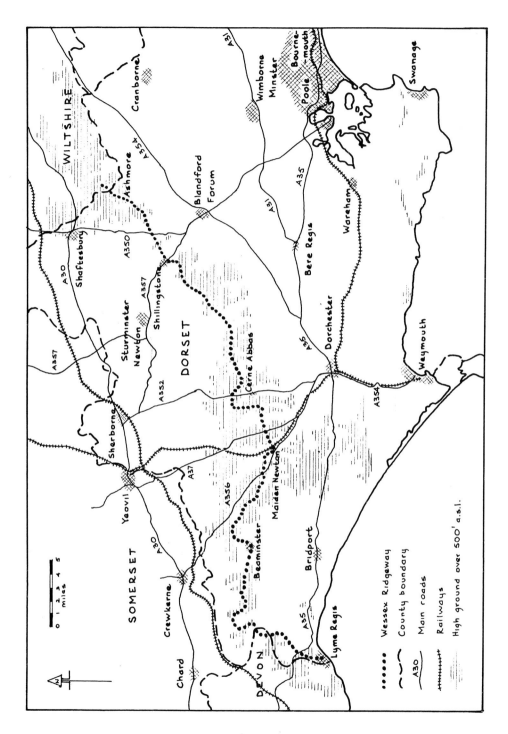

WILTSHIRE

Cranborne

A31

Bourne-mouth

Wimborne Minster

Poole

Swanage

Ashmore

A354

Blandford Forum

A31

A35

Wareham

Shaftesbury

A30

A350

Sturminster Newton

A357

Shillingston

Bere Regis

DORSET

A357

A352

Cerne Abbas

Dorchester

Weymouth

A35

A354

Sherborne

A357

Yeovil

A37

Maiden Newton

SOMERSET

A30

A356

Beaminster

Bridport

Crewkerne

DEVON

A35

Lyme Regis

Chard

0 1 2 3 4 5
miles

N

Wessex Ridgeway
County boundary
A30   Main roads
Railways
High ground over 500' a.s.l.

8

NOTES ON MAPS

The maps in this guide are diagrammatic only. They are not drawn to scale and even their proportions vary according to the need to show helpful detail. This is necessary because the paths are mostly not waymarked and may are not (yet!) signposted. Not *all* stiles and gates are shown. Serious walkers will doubtless wish to follow their steps on real maps as well and a list follows. The new OS numbering for Pathfinder maps has been used, with the old, helpful and familiar numbers in brackets

Pathfinder - 1:25 000 (East to West)

1281 (ST.81/91) - Shillingstone/Tollard Royal
1300 (ST.80/90) - Blandford Forum
1299 (ST.60/70) - Cerne Abbas/Hazelbury Bryan
1318 (SY.69/79) - Dorchester North/Tolpuddle
1317 (SY.49/59) - Bridport
1298 (ST.40/50) - Crewkerne/Beaminster
1297 (ST.20/30) - Chard
1316 (SY. 29/39) - Lyme Regis/Axminster

Landranger - 1:50 000 (East to West)

Sheet 184 - Salisbury and the Plain
195 - Bournemouth and Purbeck (a minute corner)
194 - Dorchester and Weymouth
193 - Taunton and Lyme Regis

PART 1
THE WESSEX RIDGEWAY

Section I. ASHMORE to SHILLINGSTONE - 9½ miles
(Pathfinder ST.81/91.1281)

You enter Dorset by a stile in the hedge between two fields at GR.916979 and walk straight ahead along the left hand edge of the second field to the road.

A   You are now in Ashmore Village (Note 1). Turn right and walk up to the famous Ashmore pond. Walk along its right hand side and turn left at the T-junction. Continue along the road, round a slight left-hand bend, past a farm on your right and then some cottages.

B   At some white railings, turn left into a wide-entranced stony lane marked "Bridleway only - No motors". Pause to look at the view over the left-hand gate. The Isle of Wight can be seen on a clear day.

Follow the lane south for about a mile and a quarter. After a small spinney on the left you reach a track crossing. Keep straight on, round the bar and into Ashmore wood. After about 300 yards you reach a crossing. Take the second left, i.e. signed bridleway which goes off east at right angles. This leads to a T-junction at the end of the wood where you will be turning right.

Before turning, stop and have a look at the view. Straight ahead and behind the green hill is the Tarrant valley. Over to the left is Farnham with Cranborne Chase beyond. To the right, and beyond Harbins Park, is the Stour valley.

C   Then turn right and walk down the edge of the wood for half a mile, descending into a narrow valley with a track running along it. This is Stubhampton Bottom.

D   Turn right and walk along the bottom for a short distance watching out to your left for a small signpost saying "Footpath" and pointing to a tiny path. Turn into this and follow its winding route uphill to emerge into a large field. Keep straight on, following the right hand headland round the field and out onto the road. Turn right and follow the road uphill for about a quarter mile.

E   After passing a bridleway sign "To Pimperne" on your left, keep going until the wood on your left is about to come to an end. (GR.891144) Then turn into the wood by a gate standing back from the road on the left. Follow the path down inside the wood for about ½ mile until it opens out into a clearing. This little corner rejoices in the strange name of "Heth" but all becomes clear when you learn that this is derived from "haeth" the Old English word for "heath". At the far end of the clearing, ignore a tempting track going off to the right and keep straight on, along a now barely visible little path until you emerge into an open field. Turn right and follow the headland up the field and out onto a road.

Cross the road with a sharp left/right, taking the second gate onto a stony track. Follow this through the wood for the best part of a mile and, when you emerge onto Preston Hill, stop and look round. Ahead you can see your next objective, Hambledon Hill, with the two spurs leading up to it from the east with a wood between. Down to your left is a rolling pattern of slope and valley with Ranston Hill at the far end.

F   Continue along the track until it bends sharp left. Then leave it and go straight ahead to the stile facing you. Walk downhill along the right-hand headland of four fields to the road. Pause at the start of the second field to have another look at Hambledon and now, by following the horizon round to the left, you can also catch a glimpse of the northern edge of Hod Hill.

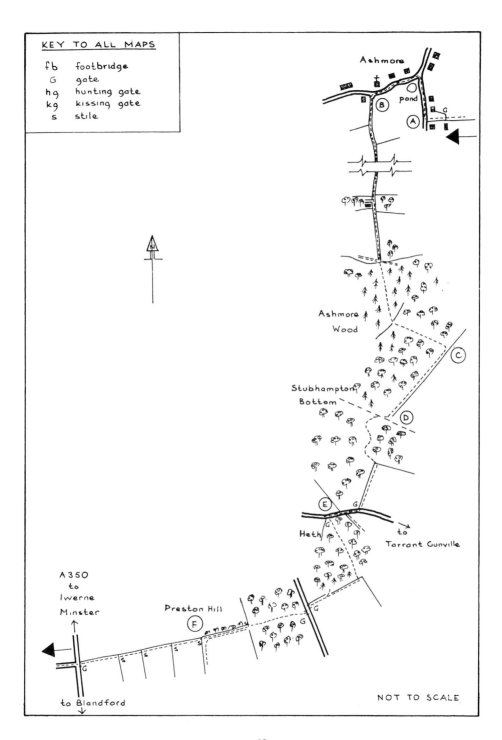

KEY TO ALL MAPS

fb	footbridge
G	gate
hg	hunting gate
kg	kissing gate
s	stile

Ashmore

pond

B

A

G

Ashmore
Wood

C

Stubhampton
Bottom

D

E   G

Heth

to
Tarrant Gunville

A350
to
Iwerne
Minster

Preston Hill

F

G

G

to Blandford

NOT TO SCALE

A Cross the road - carefully as it is the main A350 Blandford/Shaftesbury road and the traffic is very fast. Having crossed, continue straight ahead along the minor road. This brings you into Shroton (Note 2).

B When you reach a crossroads, turn half left to a lane and, after a few yards, follow the three-sided diversion round a private garden and back onto the lane. This soon becomes a wide grass strip along the back gardens of some terraced houses (whose friendly occupants keep it mown for us!).

When the green track debouches onto a road, bear left to a gate and stile on your right, signposted "Steepleton Corner and Child Okeford". Over the stile and walk diagonally left up a green track. This soon merges into a farm track which you follow for about 150 yards to a gate. Go through this and turn right at once, climbing up a stony track for about half a mile to the trig point at the top. (C on the map) (GR.848123)

It is worth leaving the route here for an hour to explore Hambledon Hill Fort (Note 3). To do so, turn right at the trig point and follow the fenced bridleway downhill and through a small wooden gate. Continue along the track for a further 300 yards and you will see a gap in the ramparts to your left. This is one of the original gateways to the hillfort and you can walk through and up into the centre. Having explored, return to the trig point the same way.

C If you have not taken the digression, continue from the trig point. Turn left and follow the fence down to the corner by a wood and round to the right, into a fenced path leading to a hunting-gate.

D The gate leads into a large field, with a track coming towards you and turning left along the top edge. If you are going to diverge here to visit Hod Hill (see Footnote) you would turn left here, along the top of the field. Otherwise keep straight on with the fence on your right to the next gate at E.

E There is a plethora of gates here. Go through the one in front of you and keep straight on, nearly to the bottom corner. Cut this and continue left along a fence with a scrubby hedge beside it. At the end of the field, go through a gate and turn half right into a fenced track running steeply downhill with a wood on the right.

At the end of the track, turn through the gate into the wood and follow the winding, muddy track down to the road where you will turn left.

FOOTNOTE:

To visit Hod Hill, follow the track along the top from D, with a wood to your left for about half a mile until you come to a barn. Follow the track round the barn and downhill, along the right headland of a field, to the road. Turn right and walk down the road for about 200 yards, then cross to a very muddy space in the trees on the other side. Take the path leading up to the left, through a hunting gate, then turn right and walk up to the gate and stile leading into the fort.

Return down to the road the same way and turn left. Follow the road for half a mile until you reach the turning point down to Hanford School and Forge. Here you rejoin the main route at F on the map (GR.846114) and continue from A overleaf.

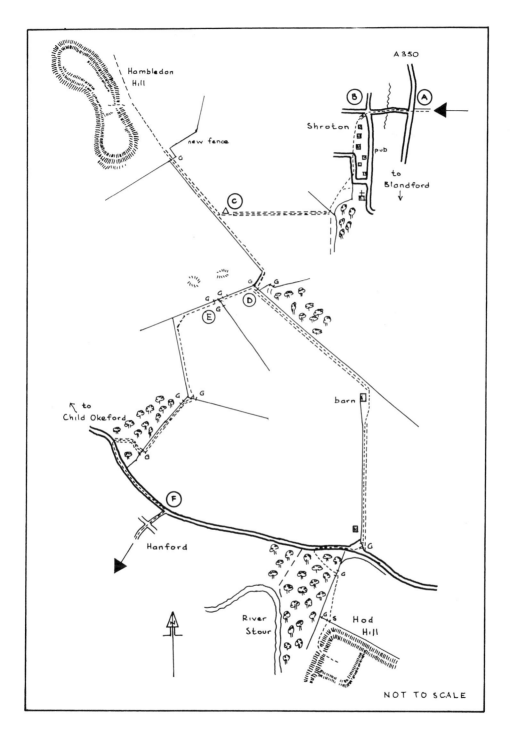

Hambledon Hill

A 350

B

Shroton

pub

A

to Blandford
↓

new fence

G

C

△

G G

G G

D

E

G

↗ to
Child Okeford

G

barn

G

F

Hanford

G

River Stour

G s

Hod Hill

NOT TO SCALE

15

A   Turn left along the road for about 400 yards to a lane forking back on your right, signposted variously: "School", "No Through Road", and "Hanford Farms". Follow it down to a Y junction; fork right and continue to a large board announcing "Hanford Farms". On the way you will catch glimpses of the seventeenth century Hanford House - now a school - and of the little church, also seventeenth century.

Just past the sign-board there is a bridleway sign at the entrance to a field on your right. Go through and cross the field diagonally left to the gate in the opposite corner. Through that, cross to the gate ahead and walk up the next field with the fence on your left. At the end, leave by the gate across the farm track to a second gate opposite and follow the headland, with the fence on your right, to the wood at the far end. Enter the wood, turn left and follow the winding path to the end. The exit gate is a few yards down to the right and brings you out into a short track leading down into an open field.

B   Over to the left you can see the bridge over the Stour. Make your way to it ready to cross. The bridge has been constructed on the site of an ancient Roman ford and many people think that it will have been the spot where the original Ridgeway crossed the Stour. From the bridge you can see your next gate - quarter-left ahead. Go through it and follow the muddy lane under the old railway line and out onto the A354 at Shillingstone (Note 5). (GR.832106)

Section II. SHILLINGSTONE to GIANTS HEAD - 13 miles
(Pathfinders ST.81/91,80/90,60/70 - 1281,1300,1299)

C   Emerge from the lane onto the A357, cross the road, turn right and walk along for a few yards to the far end of a row of Council houses. Go through a gap in the hedge here and walk up the left hand edge of the field.

Out onto the road, turn left and follow the road for about 300 yards, ignoring a left turn and passing on your right an old quarry embellished with picnic tables. This is White Pit which was cleared and made into an attractive picnic site by the local Boy Scouts a few years ago.

D   Just beyond White Pit, take the path half right which runs up the hill and follow it to open ground at the top. Here you have two alternatives:

EITHER turn right and follow the stony track to the right. This curves round to the left for about 300 yards to a gate over which you can spot a Trig point. (E)

OR take a very worthwhile digression into the middle of the field by going through the gate ahead and walking up and straight across the field, aiming between a pair of little treetops to the left on the horizon and a single one to the right. This brings you to a bridleway crossing in the centre. Stop here to look back at the view across the Stour - the last time you will see it. Then turn right and follow the uncultivated bridleway past a Trig point and out through a gateway onto a grass ride. Turn left and you have now joined the other route. (E)

The ride continues along the edge for another 300 yards (ignoring the first right fork) and then opens out into a wide, grassy space. The track you are on continues straight ahead and another forks half right. Follow the latter which cuts through the wood and out into the open where it becomes a stony lane. Walk down this, across the road and straight up the lane on the other side at F. (GR.813093)

16

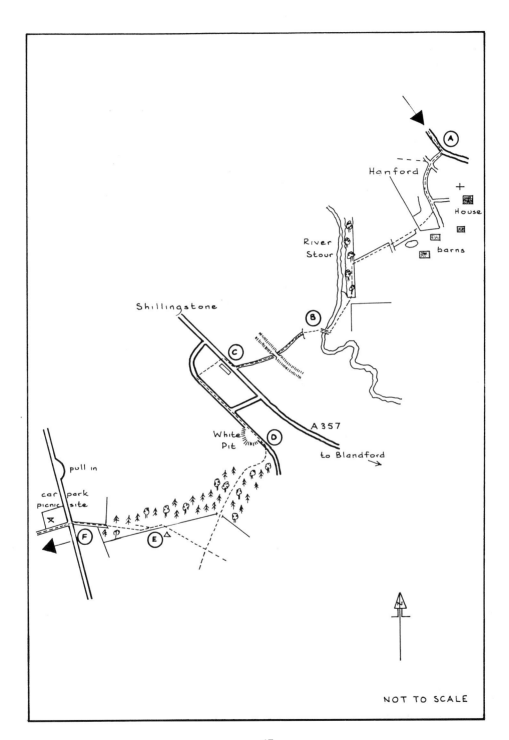

A

Hanford

River
Stour

House

barns

Shillingstone

B

C

A 357

White
Pit

D

to Blandford

pull in

car park
picnic site

F

E

NOT TO SCALE

A   There is a car park-cum-picnic site on the corner here and it would be worth your while to walk past this up the road to the crest of the hill where, from a little pull-in on the right, you will get a rather splendid view over the Blackmoor Vale and across to Hambledon on your right. Then back to the lane and walk up it leaving the car park to your right. Halfway up the hill you will see direction signs to another picnic site down to the right. Again it would be worth crossing the field into this as it affords a splendid panorama of Blackmoor Vale from the edge of the down.

B   About ¾ mile from the road crossing watch out for a National Trust sign on your left indicating the Roman-British settlement of Ringmoor (Note 6). Go in, passing a lovely old pond at the entrance, and walk along the top, then half left downhill to see the earthworks.

    Returning to your track, which now changes from stony to muddy, continue uphill for another half-mile to the top. This ridge is called Bell Hill. Here another track comes in from the left, joining yours beside a small Post Office mast and a little hut. Keep straight on downhill, along a stony track, out onto the road and turn left. (GR.794078)

C   You now have about 1 ½ miles of road walking before you, along the top of the ridge of Ibberton and Woolland Hills. You can mitigate this to a certain extent and obtain a better view across the Vale by traversing the Ibberton Hill picnic site which is on the left just after Baker's Folly, the only building on the whole ridge - so called because it had no water supply until the late 1970s and all water had to be carted. It is now a restaurant occasionally providing meals and cream teas. (See Footnote)

    After the picnic site, keep along the right hand side of the road from where you can see the sweep of Chitcombe Down below. It is now a private, experimental nature reserve where there is some hope of negotiating a permissive path along the top of the down.

D   When you reach the viewing spot at Delcombe Head, (GR.784059) it is worth stepping between the cars to look at the topography as you are now on Bulbarrow Hill, the second highest in the country. Its name derives from an Old English word meaning "hill". To get down to Milton Abbas for the night from here, see Walk No. 5.

    At the far end of the viewing site, take the right fork at the flat crossroads, signposted to Stoke Wake and Mappowder, keeping along the top edge of the down and ignoring a left turn. Half a mile later, keep straight on along the road signposted Stoke Wake and Mappowder, ignoring the right turn down to Woolland. A few yards from here you have an unparalleled view down onto Rawlesbury Camp (Note 7) with its interesting green humps and bumps. The remains of a wooden cross on a little hump denotes the site of a great interdenominational open air service held each year in the 60s and 70s.

E   A few yards later you will see a gate in the fence on your left leading to a green track into the camp. Follow this into the camp, enjoy the view from the cross and leave by the little path on the lower rampart below it. This leads you along the edge, through a hunting-gate in the trees and right round to the other side of the camp. Now turn left and, keeping a small wood on your right, walk straight ahead, down through a gate and down a steep slope to a second gate at F. (GR.764055) From here you can, if you wish, walk down to Ansty for refreshment or for the night. (See Walk No.4)

    FOOTNOTE: If wanting to eat at Baker's Folly, telephone first to Philips - 0258-817582

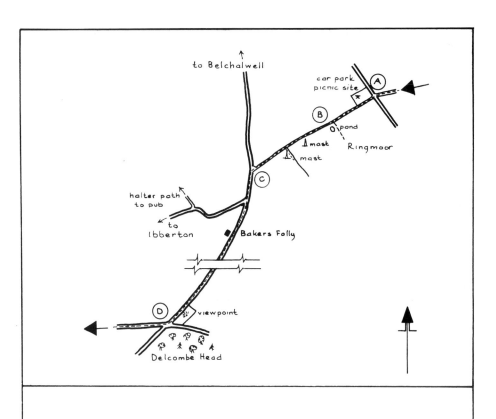

to Belchalwell

car park
picnic site

(A)

(B)

pond

mast

mast

Ringmoor

(C)

halter path
to pub

to
Ibberton

Bakers Folly

(D) viewpoint

Delcombe Head

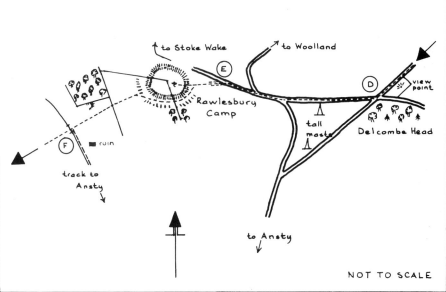

to Stoke Wake

to Woolland

(E)

Rawlesbury
Camp

(D) view point

tall
masts

Delcomba Head

(F) ruin

track to
Ansty

to Ansty

NOT TO SCALE

19

A   Otherwise keep straight on down to another pair of gates. Here you go through the right hand one and follow the left hand hedge down a long narrow field. When the field narrows still further - to half its width - follow the wired-in path along the right hand side, entered by a bar stile. A few yards after negotiating two more bar stiles, you cross a stream by a footbridge which brings you to the start of a muddy lane.

B   Walk to the end of the lane, cross the road and continue on the (very muddy) lane on the other side, passing the buildings of Crockers Farm on your right. The origin of its name is probably an Old English word meaning "potter". Where the track divides, keep right and go through the gate. Cross the next two fields diagonally left, gate to gate. Entering the third field, walk straight across and follow the far hedge left, and left again, to the gate on your right into the NW corner of Breach Wood. Go in and follow the narrow path through to the far end.

C   You emerge into a large, untidy open space with a tarmac road coming in from the left and a lane going straight ahead with a barn on the right. (GR.753039). Walk up this lane to Melcombe Park Farm. Just before the farmhouse, turn right onto the concrete road running in front of it; pass several barns on your right; go through the right hand one of the three gates at the end of the barns and turn right. Walk along the bottom of the slope, parallel to Hill Wood on your right, and go through the hunting gate at the end of the field.

D   Now keep straight on, along the top of the slope down to your right, keeping an eye out to the left for a green track going in your direction. Cross over to this and follow it down to a gate which leads you into the Dorsetshire Gap (Note 8). Since 1972 there has been a book in the Gap which it is the custom for visitors to sign. This was started by a writer known as "Valesman" who left there, in his sandwich tin, a notebook he happened to have with him because he felt this might help to preserve the Gap. A book is now kept in a tin box which you will find on your right as you enter. Please sign it.

E   To leave the Gap turn hard back left downhill, signposted Higher Melcombe. After 20 yards or so you meet another track coming down on your right. Turn up this to a gate at the top, through it and keep straight on along a green track.

OR leave by a new path signposted 'Folly'. This leads round the base of a high knoll, up through the wood to its edge, and left down to the gate onto the green track. This is the path which will be waymarked and is now the preferred route. It is shown in the map on page 65.

This track comes to an end beside a depression on your left which was once a dew-pond. Keeping this on your left, go forward for a few yards to a hunting gate. Go through and walk ahead, aiming at and passing a small water tower (GR.738029) at F on the map opposite. At the end of the field you hit a tree belt, at right angles to your path, with a narrow path running down inside it. Turn right into this and walk down to a gate. Go through this and continue downhill with the fence on your left. Follow the track round to the right when the field to the left comes to an end and continue down the track until it reaches the road. This is Folly (Note 9).

G   Cross the road and walk up the track on the other side. This ends in a gate which you go through, continuing up the right hand side of two fields, to the entrance to a wood - Watcombe Wood. This takes its name from Watcombe Botton, below on your left, and means "Valley where wheat is grown" from the Old English.

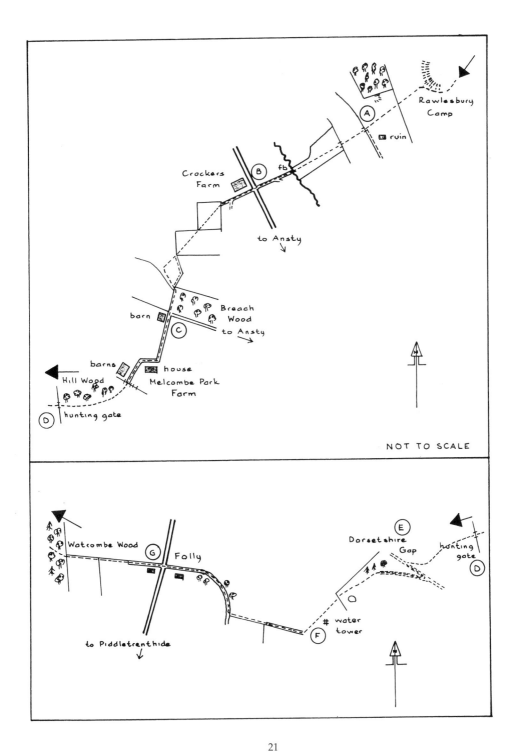

NOT TO SCALE

A Enter the wood, turn right and walk through it and out into an open field. This is Church Hill. Walk ahead, past an old dew-pond ruined by cattle, to explore the remains of an old settlement at GR.716036. Little is known of this but as the bridleway you are following was once a drove road, the settlement may have been connected. It is believed to be medieval.

Leaving the settlement, cross over to the hedge on your right and continue to walk along its left hand side through the next field, then through a short, uncultivated strip with a barn in it. Pass the barn on your right and keep the same line through the next two fields. In the last one watch out for a tumulus half left ahead and a white house below you.

B This is your signal to continue to the corner of the field and turn left down the hedge, ignoring the gate in front of you. Halfway down the hill, go through a gate in the hedge on your right and walk down a green drove along the left had side of the hedge. This brings you out onto the road about half a mile north of Alton Pancras (meaning "Farm at the source of a stream" - Old English; in this case, the source of the River Piddle.)

C A few yards to the left you can see a lane going off on the other side of the road. Walk up this for a yard or two, then leave it passing a barn on your right, and fork left up a hedged drove. Follow this to the top and continue on the same line, with the hedge on your left, through the next two fields. At the end of the second field there is a large barn on the other side of the hedge to your left. Known as Black Barn, it is a useful local landmark and a four-way bridleway crossing. White owls have been known to nest in the barn.

D Leaving the Barn and the gate into it on your left, continue in the same direction along the right hand side of the hedge through two more fields. At the top of the second one, go through a hunting gate, turn right and walk along the hedge to the stile at the far end. This brings you into the Giants Head Caravan Park (Note 13). If not staying here for the night you can either continue or walk down to Cerne Abbas (Note 11) for food/accommodation. To do this, carry on from the caravan site as described below and turn left at the end of the first field. Then follow the marked footpath down to Cerne.

Section III. GIANTS HEAD TO MAIDEN NEWTON - 8¾ miles
(Pathfinders ST.60/70, SY.69/79 - 1299, 1318)

E Emerging from the caravan site, cross the road, enter the field on the other side and walk down the field diagonally right to a gap through into the next field. Cross this on the same line to a gate into a lightly wooded strip. Here you follow a faint green track ahead for about 30 feet when it curves down to the right. Leave it when it climbs uphill, drop down to the gate on the left and out into a cultivated field.

F Looking diagonally right across this field you can see a projecting field corner with a single tree in it at GR.669032. Walk down towards this, go through the gate and turn along the track on the other side, with the hedge on your left. Continue along the track as it curves to the right, along the right hand side of a beech hedge. When you reach a lane crossing, turn left, passing a farm on your right. This is Minterne Parva. As the lane turns, watch out for a small round building up on your left. This is believed locally to have been a cockfighting ring - probably eighteenth century. On the corner in front of it is the base of an old village cross.

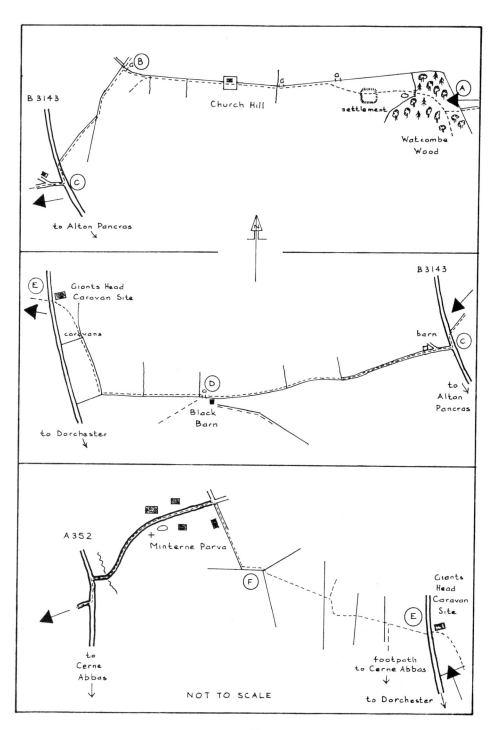

B 3143

Church Hill

settlement

Watcombe Wood

B 3143

to Alton Pancras

N

Giants Head Caravan Site

caravans

to Dorchester

D

Black Barn

barn

C

to Alton Pancras

A 352

Minterne Parva

F

Giants Head Caravan Site

E

footpath to Cerne Abbas

to Cerne Abbas

to Dorchester

NOT TO SCALE

A The lane brings you out onto the A352 main road from Sherborne to Dorchester. Turn left, walk along it for 150 yards and take the first right, signposted "Up Cerne". This takes you into Up Cerne itself (Note 12). At the crossing leading to the church turn right, along the right hand side of a tile-topped wall. You are walking along a made-up farm road, alongside a clear chalk stream which descends through a series of man-made lakes below Up Cerne, into the River Cerne itself.

Follow the farm road up the valley for about half a mile as it goes up and down, finally turning left uphill, leaving only a grass track ahead. (GR.653035)

B Follow the lane left and up, through a double-hedged section and then along a wide grass and stone track, to a large tree circle at the top. As the track veers left, leave it at the first tree on your right, turning right and walking straight across the field. Half way across, aim to the left of two trees on the far sky line sticking up like a large umbrella. This brings you to a gap in the hedge at the end of the field.

C Once through the hedge, turn right onto a very narrow path through the gorse and brambles until you hit a lane coming in from the right which becomes a wide cart track continuing to your left. Turn left onto this. You are going to follow this track south, imperceptibly downhill, for about 2 miles along Gore Hill, where you now are, Redpost Hill, Ball's Hill, Buckland Hill and Cowdown Hill. Down to your left is the Cerne Valley and to your right the Sydling Valley.

After the first 100 yards, ignore a left fork turning into a field and keep straight on, aiming at a small communications mast. Just after passing a slight rise on your left, keep a look-out there for the ditch and bank of the Cerne Park Pale. This formerly enclosed one of the 90 or so deer parks which members of the nobility and clergy established for themselves in Dorset after the Norman Conquest. Along this section of the track you may also be able to spot through the gap in the left hand edge the faint outline of the famous Cerne Giant carved in the slope facing you across the Cerne Valley. Eventually the track becomes a stony lane and ends at a road.

D Cross the road and continue down the headland of the next field - now a stony track leading to a vast new barn, with another behind it. Turn right at the end of the field, between the second barn and the hedge. Keeping the hedge on your left, walk up the field and through the tree clump (whence Field Farm Barn (E), hitherto a landmark on all OS maps, has vanished). Continue on the track down the next field and round left/right onto the ridge. (GR.642997) Here you have a splendid view across the Sydling Valley to the Break Heart Hill on the far side - which you will soon be climbing.

F You can EITHER continue diagonally left, over a stile and on down to the gate in the corner OR, if the field is under crop and as you cannot see the gate from the top, you can turn left, walk along the top of the field into the next one, turn right and go down the left had side of the hedge to the same spot.

Either way you find yourself on a very attractive piece of downland dropping down to the right. Stay at the top and follow a green track round the slope, and in the same direction round the next field and out onto a lane.

G Turn right along this and follow it round to the right at the bottom of the hill. This is Sydling St Nicholas (Note 13).

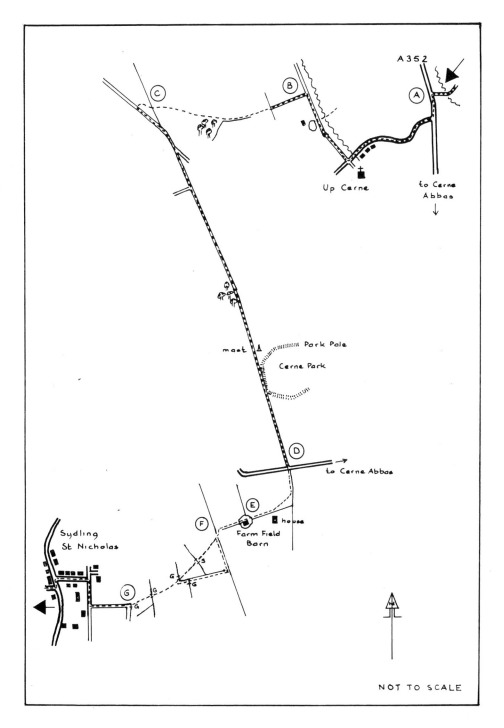

A352

to Cerne
Abbas

Up Carne

to Cerne Abbas

meet ⌂ ⋯⋯ Park Pale

Cerne Park

■ house

Sydling
St Nicholas

Farm Field
Barn

NOT TO SCALE

25

A   About 100 yards along the flat, turn left past the front of the older houses and out onto the main road. Turn right along this for the pub, otherwise cross it left/right and turn up the lane towards the church, passing a gabled house on your right and a spectacular Chestnut tree on your left. (GR. 632994)

B   Follow the lane round to the right - leaving the church on your left - and then round to the left as it starts to climb. When it emerges from the trees, veer right along a hedged grass track. After about 150 yards this curves left and climbs again, ending at a gate. Go through and keep straight on up until you reach a gate in the hedge on your left with a lone ash tree beside it. Go through into the adjoining field, turn right and continue up it and the next field, in the same direction only now with the hedge on your right.

C   At the top (of Break Heart Hill) you emerge onto the A37 Dorchester/Yeovil road and walk straight along the lane on the other side. This ends at some barns. Pause to admire the view across the Frome Valley and then pass the barns on your right, follow the curve to the left and take to the stony farm road running downhill. This ends at a gate. Go through and turn right down a lane which takes you down, past the railway station and into Maiden Newton (Note 14).

Section IV. MAIDEN NEWTON TO BEAMINSTER - 10¼ miles
(Pathfinders SY.49/59, ST.40/50 - 1317,1298)

D   If continuing on through Maiden Newton, turn left at the bottom of the lane after passing the railway station. Follow the road round until it curves to the left, then leave it for the open space by the church containing the War Memorial on your right. Walk to the wall ahead and turn right to walk along it, past the little gate into the churchyard on the left, and into the farmyard at the end.

Before the farm buildings on your left you will see a gate with a stile beside it. Go through and turn right to follow the top of the green bank which slopes down to the River Frome on your left . Towards the far end of the meadow watch out for a muddy path which forks left down to the river. Clamber down this and turn right along the bottom to the footbridge.

E   Cross the footbridge, turn right and follow the clearly defined path along the Frome, under the railway bridge and passing two field boundaries coming in on your left. This part of the walk is taking you along what were once water-meadows and in places you can still see remains of the old channels, bridges and sluices.

F   Just before the end of the third field - where a tributary of the Frome will cross your route - turn left and walk up the hedge to the top of the field. Go over the wooden bars in the fence ahead and walk right and left along the hedge to a ladder stile (or horse jump!) on your right. Negotiate this and walk straight across the field to a gate on the far side, then straight across again to a second gate to the right of the church (G on the map). (GR.591988)

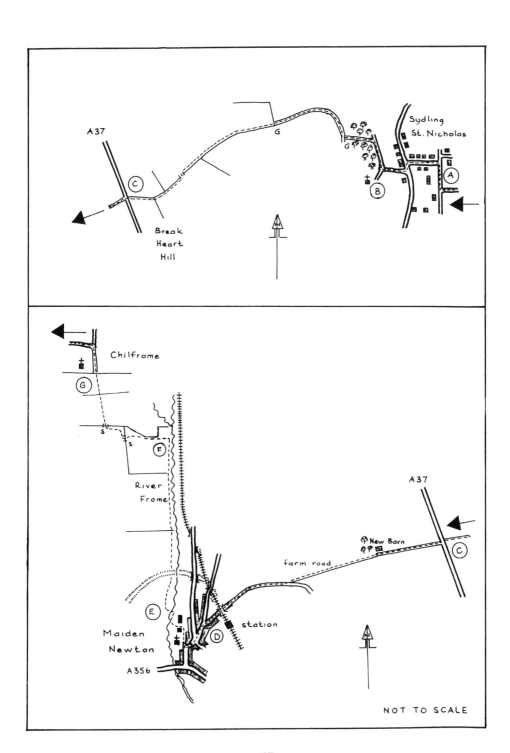

A37

Sydling
St. Nicholas

C

G

A

B

Break
Heart
Hill

Chilfrome

G

s

s

F

River
Frome

A37

New Barn

C

farm road

E

station

D

Maiden
Newton

A356

NOT TO SCALE

A   This leads you into a lane which curves round the church on your left and out onto the road. You are now in Chilfrome. According to the Domesday Book, the estate at that time belonged jointly to three thegns, which accounts for the village's name - from Old English "cild" meaning 'noble born son'.

Ignore the road to your right and walk straight ahead for about 350 yards to a crossroads. Turn right, up the lane signposted "Grove Stall Farm". About 350 yards up the hill, the high bank on your left comes to an end. Here you take the left turn, along a narrow lane curving away round the edge of the hill. This brings you out onto the road where you continue straight ahead in the same direction.

B   Unfortunately you now have to walk along this road for about 1½ miles, passing Higher Chilfrome and Lancombe Farms on your right, until it meets the A356 Crewkerne/Dorchester road at a T-junction. Turn left and walk along the A356 for about 200 yards. Watch the numbered poles along the left hand side of the road and, just after No. 28, go through the gate into the field on your right. (GR.564989)

C   Turn half right and cross the field, aiming at the left hand end of the high hedge on the horizon until you spot the gate a little to the right. Go through and walk straight across the second field, aiming slightly to the left of four upstanding trees in the far hedge. Here you will spot a narrow little path curving down through some scrub to a hunting gate. Go through and follow the same line through two or more fields, following the top of the slope in the first and cutting the corner to a hunting gate in the second. Go through and walk down beside the tree-shrouded ditch on your left until this comes to an end. Then turn half left and aim at the solitary mid-field tree. From this, keep to the same line and aim to the right of the barn you can see in the bottom corner. When you reach it, go through a gate in the hedge on your right and turn left for 12 yards, then right and walk along the muddy lane into Lower Kingcombe. (D)

The Lower Kingcombe Estate of 600 acres had not been broken up for 400 years until May 1987 when it was put up for auction in 15 lots. Its unsprayed fields and meadows have been described as a "unique survival" in Southern England and 240 acres of the Estate are included in a S.S.I. Until 1987 the village was entirely deserted and to walk through it was to step back into the Middle Ages. A public appeal, supported by the District Council and the Nature Conservancy Council, enabled the Dorset Trust for Nature Conservation to buy 320 acres. Life is now returning to the village and a Field Centre has been set up there. (See Accommodation List)

E   At the top of the village the road veers left. Leave it here, enter the hollow lane ahead and walk up this for about half a mile until it emerges, through a hunting gate, into a field.

F   Walk straight on across the field to the hunting gate into the bottom of the wood ahead (Kingcombe Coppice) and follow the path ahead for a couple of hundred yards. Another hunting gate at the far end brings you out into a field. Here you follow the valley ahead round, through a hunting gate and then up to a field gate onto a road facing a forest of gigantic masts. This is Rampisham Down and the masts are part of the BBC's Overseas Broadcasting Service.

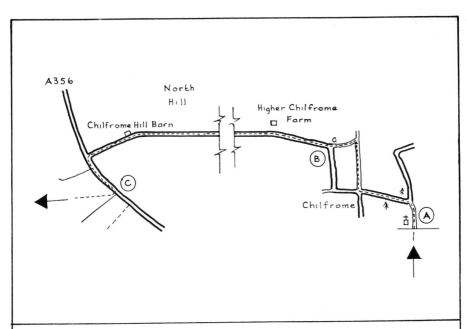

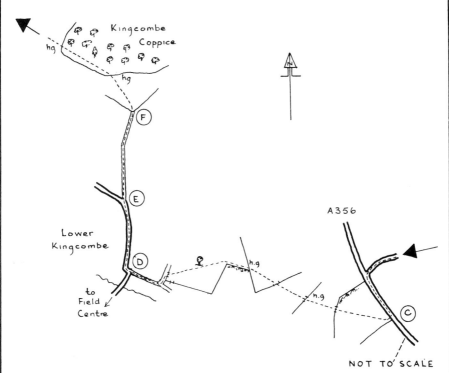

A   Turn right onto the road for a few yards and then, where it veers right, turn left into a stony lane at GR.549007. After about 200 yards the lane ends at a gate but you go through this and continue in the same direction for another 200 yards, keeping the hedge on your right.

B   As the ground drops, go through the hunting gate ahead and turn half left. You are looking down across a valley and your target is a gate beside a single tree part way up the far side. If you walk down and up to this and go through the gate, you will find yourself in what must once have been an old, hollow lane as it is sunk between a hedge on the left and a bank on the right. Follow it round to the left, on through a gap into the next field and down to a road. This is Chalk Corner and the hill up to your right was Rampisham Hill.

C   Cross the road and walk straight down the hollow lane on the other side. This brings you down to Hooke Village, past a footbridge and a fish farm. Turn left at a big white house and walk a few yards along a road to a T-junction. Here you turn right and continue along the road through the village, passing Hooke Court, which is now St. Francis' School, on your left. If you intend to explore Hooke Park (Note 15), keep straight along the road here. Turn right at the end and you will find the entrance on the left a few yards on.

D   Otherwise take the next field gate on your right just after Hooke Court, (GR.530004) and cross the field diagonally up to the left-hand end of the wood on the far side. Then cross the stile and follow the contour along to your left, keeping the wood close to your right until it thins to a hedge. After a few yards you will see a large gap in the hedge. Turn right, through the gap, and walk down the next field, parallel to the road below to the left, and out onto this at first field gate. Turn right and walk up the road.

E   The most direct route from here is to follow the road uphill for 1¼ miles until you reach a large open space on your right. Then fork right, aiming at a group of tall firs on the horizon, and follow a narrow track which brings you out at Dirty Gate on the B1363 Beaminster road.

However, there is a far pleasanter route, and only a fraction longer. Walk up the road for about 100 yards and take the right turn to Toller Whelme. This takes you nearly a mile along a pleasant valley, passing two lakes on the left, occupied on some days by a flock of Canada geese. Keep left at the third house, Lake Farm (East Farm on OS map), and then go through the gate ahead on the left which takes you onto the tarmac drive past the front of Toller Manor.

Toller Whelme (Note 16) takes its name from the Old English "aewielm" meaning "a river spring" and is the source of the river Hooke whose old name was Toller.

F   *After passing the Manor, and then West Farm, round to your right, the drive goes round to the right but you keep straight on - along a stony/grassy track. This takes you past a ruined building and then an old concrete prefabricated structure on you right, and then through a gate into a field. Walk straight on, along the left hand edge of this field and the next one, and out onto a road. This is the B3163 and you turn left and walk 100 yards along it to Dirty Gate. Exhaustive research has so far failed to unearth the reason for this name, but enquiries are still in progress!*

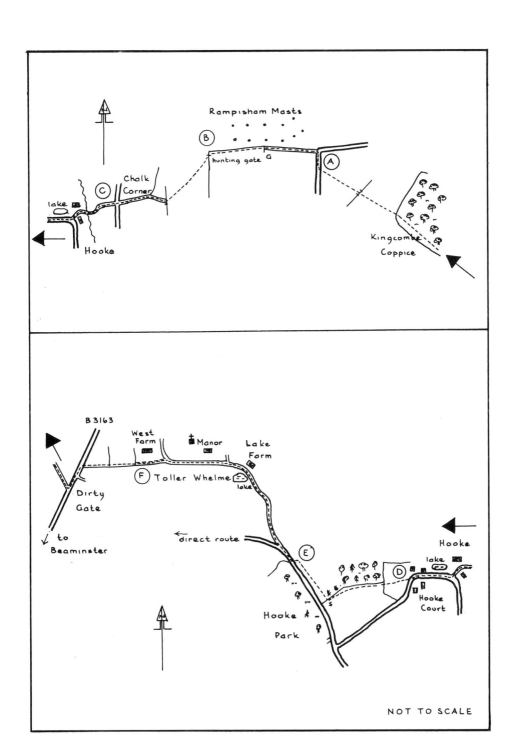

Rampisham Masts

(B)

hunting gate

(A)

Chalk
Corner

(C)

lake

Kingcombe
Coppice

Hooke

B 3163

West
Farm

Manor

Lake
Farm

(F) Toller Whelme

lake

Dirty
Gate

direct route

Hooke

↓ to
Beaminster

(E)

lake

(D)

Hooke
Court

Hooke ⚑ -

Park

NOT TO SCALE

31

A   Take the lane running north signposted "Langdon - No Through Road" and just keep going up and along the ridge for a mile and a half, passing from lane to track and gazing across to Toller Down on the right and down to Beaminster on the left. Towards the top, cross a minor road straight into the field opposite and walk up the left-hand edge to the next road. Turn left and follow the road for about a half a mile. This is Mintern's hill and the road along the ridge is thought to have been part of the original Ridgeway route.

B   Just after a right turn - which you ignore - watch out for a picnic sign on your left and turn down the lane beside it, leaving the picnic area on your right (GR.485035). This is Stinford Lane which, half a mile later and just past a house called "Ebeneezer", turns into a road. This little area is called Meerhay, meaning "Enclosure by a pool".

The road you are on will take you down for about a mile into the centre of Beaminster (Note 17), sliding into a larger road just before the old school. When you get right down into the town, take the right fork at the bottom of the hill which will bring you out into the Market Square.

Section V. BEAMINSTER TO BIRDSMOORGATE - 10½ miles
(Pathfinders ST.40/50, 20/30 - 1298, 1297)

C   Leaving Beaminster by walking down the west side of the Market Square and continuing downhill as far as a pub called The Eight Bells. Turn right here and walk along Church Street, passing the church on your left and keeping the same direction when Church Street becomes Shorts Lane. Eventually the lane becomes a stony, hedged track. Follow it until it bends a sharp right, then leave it and go through the gate in front of you.

D   Here you will see beside the gate a splendid stile, erected in 1985 by the Beaminster Ramblers to celebrate the Ramblers' Association Golden Jubilee. Following the same direction as before, walk along the left hand side of the field and over a stile onto the road. Turn left and then immediately right into a narrow lane and continue along this as far as the last house on your left (No. 4). Leave the road just past this and its double garage, and turn left into a narrow fenced path running alongside a vast space full of cars. Go through the gate at the end and cross the field diagonally right, aiming at the farm buildings of Higher Barrowfield in the opposite corner. Turn through the first (lower) gate and walk ahead alongside the barn. Turn left at the corner and continue up to the projecting corner of a second barn and alongside both it and the garden of the farmhouse beyond.

E   When level with the farmhouse, turn half right and walk across the field until you spot the stile in the hedge below. Over this and continue on the same line to the gateway in the next hedge. From here you should be able to see the footbridge straight ahead at the bottom of the next field (GR.467012) but, before walking down to it, look ahead and plot your line up Gerrard's Hill beyond the bridge. You will need to aim to the right of single tree in the middle of the slope in front of you, making for the hedge which runs up the hill along the right hand edge of the field.

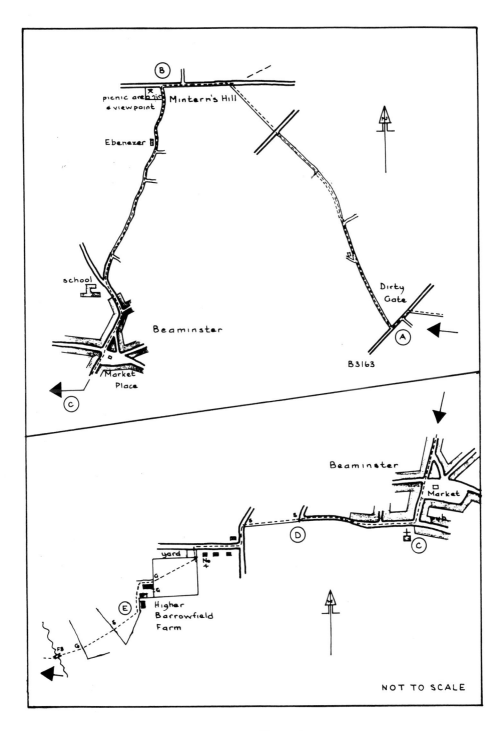

picnic area
& viewpoint

B

Mintern's Hill

Ebenezer

school

Beaminster

Dirty
Gate

A

B3163

Market
Place

C

Beaminster

Market

C

yard

D

Higher
Barrowfield
Farm

E

NOT TO SCALE

A   Now cross the footbridge, turn half right and walk up the hill to a gate in the right hand hedge. Go through, cross a track, over a stile and follow the hedge on your right to the top. Gerrard's Hill is a delightful spot with a magnificent view. In May its eastern and southern slopes are awash with wild flowers.

Leave the summit via a gate in the trees behind the trig point and follow a broad green track running straight ahead downhill, making towards the house below.

B   At the bottom of the green track, go through a gate and follow the right hand edge of a field to another gate on your right. Go through this, turn left and walk along a track, passing the houses on your left. These comprise the settlement of Chart Knolle. This is also the name of the hill you will soon pass below. Though rather a romantic name, its origin is somewhat obscure. "Knolle" is from the Old English "cnoll" meaning hillock. "Chart" may derive from a thirteenth century manorial family called Charteray.

C   Pass the houses, go through a gate and continue straight ahead along a broad, green track. This takes you along a sort of green platform round the foot of Chart Knolle first and then Waddon Hill - both up to your left. The origin of the name Waddon is of interest since it derives from Old English "wad" meaning "woad" and "dun" meaning "down" or "Hill"; i.e. the hill where woad grows. The Hill itself is topped by the remains of what is thought to have been a Roman signal station, but it is, unfortunately, privately owned and very much not open to the public.

The green track from Chart Knolle leads through a gate into a field (GR.456014). Walk along this with the hedge on your right. At the end, take the left hand of two gates and continue in the same direction through two more gates. Then your green route becomes a sandy (or muddy!) track curving downhill and to the left.

D   At the bottom, you enter a farmyard by a gate, walk straight through it and out onto a road. This is Stoke Knapp (Note 18). As you emerge from the farmyard, go straight across the road and into a lane on the opposite side. Follow this uphill, bearing round to the right and passing a National Trust sign on the left shortly after. The surface, always a bit wet and muddy, gradually changes into a mere track, curving round the base of Lewesdon hill which rises up to your left and then straightening to drop gradually down to the B3164 road at F. From D to F is about a mile and a half.

BUT

E   At E, approximately halfway between D and F, (GR.437015) you have three alternatives. At the NT sign on your left you can

EITHER continue along the route to F as above;

OR turn off right to Broadwindsor (Note 19) for refreshment or B&B, following the directions at the end of Walk No. 11 (at G on p.82);

OR climb up to explore Lewesdon Hill before continuing in either direction. Lewesdon is well worth the effort. The site of one of the Armada beacons in 1588, it affords views across three counties.

If you want to continue along the route from Lewesdon without breaking your journey at Broadwindsor, follow the path along the southern edge of the Hill and drop down to your right by a narrow path through the bracken, shortly after the NT sign at the top. Turn left onto the track at the bottom of the slope. You have now regained the main route which will bring you out onto the B3164 road.

34

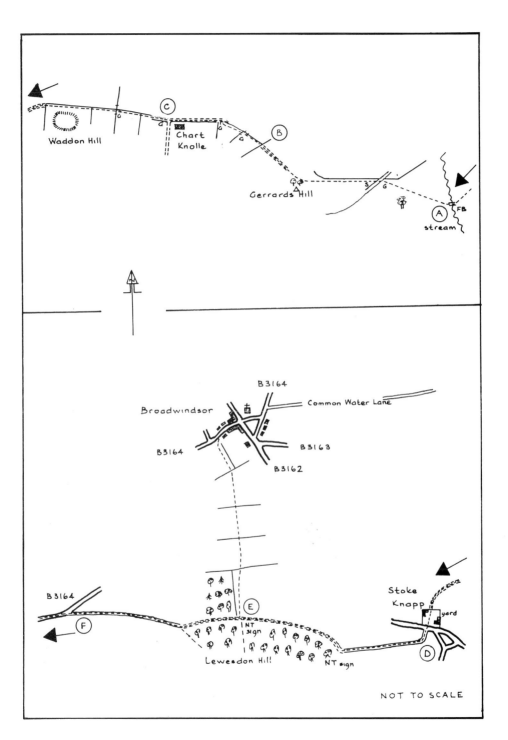

Waddon Hill

C

Chart
Knolle

B

Gerrards Hill

A

FB

stream

B3164

Broadwindsor

Common Water Lane

B3164

B3163

B3162

B3164

Stoke
Knapp

yard

E

NT
sign

F

Lewesdon Hill

NT sign

D

NOT TO SCALE

A You turn left along B3164, but it is better to cross the road first as visibility is better and you will soon be turning off to the right. After about 200 yards, turn down Sheepwash Lane which is concrete surfaced and runs back down to your right. After about 150 yards the concrete bit goes off to the left to Courtwood Farm but you keep straight on, into what is now a hedged track, muddy and stony. This drops downhill and up again and you should keep an eye out for a gate on the left at the top of the rise. It is identified by the number 2979 on its gatepost. (GR.422025)

B Go through the gate and walk diagonally left downhill, aiming at a rather thinner section of the hedge opposite. Over the stile there and then follow the right hand headland down to another stile at the bottom. Go over this, turn left and follow the farm track. This takes you through a wide gap in the hedge to a T-junction of tracks. Turn left and continue round two right hand bends to the Buildings of Lower Newnham Farm. Keep straight on, passing enormous tanks on your right, and then turn left between the buildings at the end.

C Continue along the farm track to a road, cross this and walk up the stony track ahead to the gate at the top. Go through and walk diagonally right up the next field, passing a wired-in circular concrete tank on your left. This should bring you into sight of the pair of stiles leading into Pilsdon Pen (Note 20). Negotiate them and walk up alongside the fence on your right and climb up the top bank of the Pen.

It is worth walking across to the trig point over to the left, to obtain a view of Marshwood Vale where the soil is clay and the countryside resembles that of Devon. Thomas Gerrard, in Coker's Survey of Dorset, describes it as "a little territorie called Marshwood Vale, rich and well stored with woods, by meanes whereof it affordeth convenient Dwellings", and a local way of saying "they are like chalk and cheese" is "they are as like as Lewesdon Hill and Pilsdon Pen".

D To go back to the route, if continuing after reaching the top bank from the stile, walk straight along it (i.e. the NW bank) with the open space of the Pen on your left, to the wide entrance in the far corner. Go down to the gate but do not go through it. Turn left and follow the fence downhill to a gate in front of you and go through this. (GR.410013)

E A few yards further on, go through another gate on your right and follow a track diagonally right up the hill to a third gate. Beyond this the farm track continues straight up, so leave it and continue diagonally up the field on the same line as before. This will bring you to a stile just above the far corner. Over it and turn right at once, to negotiate a second stile a few yards on. Then turn left along the top edge of the field.

(NOTE: The definitive line would be to have walked down to the eastern edge of this field and then diagonally up again to the far corner; but the landowner has kindly agreed to a permissive path along the top.)

F Once out of this field, whether you went down to the road and up again, or kept along the top, continue along the latter line, along the ridge, straight across one field and along the next one with the hedge on your right. At the end of this one the ground begins to fall slightly. Follow the hedge round to the left, passing a gate on your right, and down to the next gateway. Here you meet an earth track crossing left to right. Turn right onto this and follow it down to the road.

G Turn right and walk up the road for about 400 yards to a fork. This is Cole's Cross. Just ahead, a yard or two up the right hand fork, you go through a gate leading into a field with a steep rise on your right. Walk up this diagonally, aiming at a gate (or gap) in the hedge along the top. Turn half left and cut the left hand corner to continue along the ridge with the hedge on your left. You are now on Blackdown Hill, the name of which means "dark-coloured down".

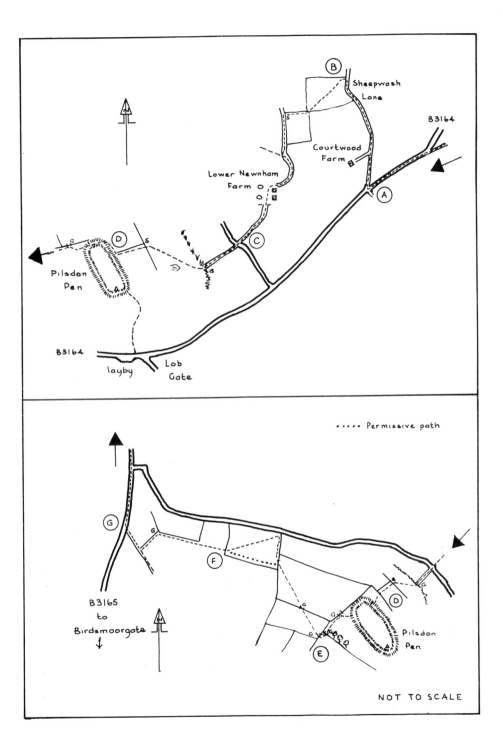

B3164

Sheepwash
Lane

B

Courtwood
Farm

Lower Newnham
Farm

A

C

D

Pilsdon
Pen

B3164

layby   Lob
         Gate

• • • • • Permissive path

G

F

D

Pilsdon
Pen

B3165
to
Birdsmoorgate

E

NOT TO SCALE

37

H   Keep the line along the ridge with hedge on your left for three more fields, and on your right in a fourth one. Then leave the hedge and walk half left downhill to a stile in the corner of the fifth field, over the stile and walk down the right hand edge of the sixth field to emerge on to the road beside a little chapel. This little corner is called Venn (from Old English "fenn" meaning fen or marshland. It is difficult to see why, since it stands fairly high above the Synderford Valley.) (GR.390040)

J   Go straight across and walk down Venn Hill along the road opposite the chapel signposted Thorncombe. After half a mile and having passed through Synderford Village, you cross the River Synderford, continue up the road for another 400 yards into the hamlet of Holway and turn left down Saddle Street.

K   The "Street" comes to an end at the farmyard of Yewtree Farm. Walk straight through the yard, leaving by a gate onto a stony track. Follow this, ignoring a left fork and a left turn and keeping straight on uphill and out into a large, cultivated field. Walk through this, and the next two fields, always keeping close the hedge on your right, and out into the road. (GR.379022)

L   Turn left for about 50 yards along the road, keeping a keen eye out for a gap in the hedge on your right with a stile on its far side. Negotiate the stile and the ditch beyond it and walk down the right hand edge of the field until you hit the farm road running along the bottom. Turn left along this to Grighay Farm. This beautiful old farmhouse was once part of the demesne of Forde Abbey. The origin of its name is not known, although "hay" derives from Old English "heag" meaning enclosure.

M   There are two choices from here. (GR.381015) The day's stint ends at Birdsmoorgate where refreshments are available at the Rose & Crown, and the landlady has a list of farmhouses offering bed and breakfast. So, if aiming at the Rose & Crown, following the route as described below[1,2] but, if you want to continue walking, turn straight to Section VI and follow the directions from A onwards.

[1]*For Birdsmoorgate walk past the Grighay farmhouse on your left and continue between a modern corrugated building and an old stone one. Then walk straight across the field, aiming at a gateway ahead with a large tree in front of it. Follow roughly the same line, round the contour, in the second field, with a wood below on your right. Do the same in the third field, clipping the hedge corner coming in to your right. This brings you to Hillview Farm - an idyllic spot.*

N   *Pass the Farm on your right and enter a very wide, fenced green track. This leads into a hedged lane running alongside what must have been an ancient road - now overgrown and alive with wild flowers. The lane continues past a few houses and down to the main road at P. Turn left and walk the quarter mile to the Rose & Crown at GR.39150095, but with some care as it is the B3165 Crewkerne/Lyme Regis road and very busy, particularly at holiday times.*

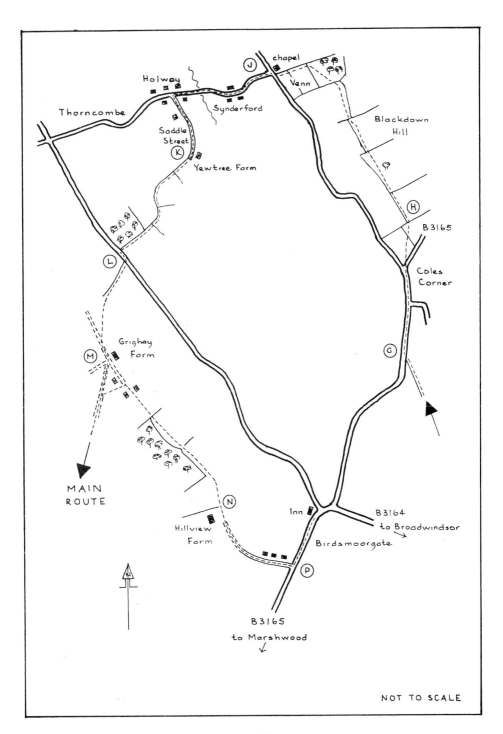

Section VI. BIRDSMOORGATE TO LYME REGIS - 10 miles
(Pathfinders ST.20/30, SY.29/39 - 1297,1316)

²Return to Grighay Farm by the same route along which you left it, going back towards the farmhouse between the old stone barn and the corrugated iron building. Then turn very hard left so that you pass below, and to the right of, a green-roofed chicken house, along a dirt track. You are now back on the main route.

A If you did not make the detour to Birdsmoorgate, pass Grighay farmhouse on your left, taking the middle path to the right of a green-roofed chicken house, along a dirt track.

The dirt track leads to a gate. Do NOT go through this, but through the one on your right. Follow the hedge on your left, past a little uncultivated enclave to the right and then aim at the left hand end of a conifer belt ahead.

B Go through the gate into the wood and follow a just discernible little path, keeping the little stream and the hedge always on your left. You may have to stray to the right occasionally when a stream crosses your path, but always come back to this left hand hedge.

Leave the wood by the gate at the far end and cross the next field diagonally right. This brings you to Gashay Farm. Go through the yard - first right, then left, and turn into the field on the left at GR.376007 just before you come to the modern farmhouse on your right. Gashay was once as beautiful as Grighay but was burned down some years ago and rebuilt in its present, unremarkable style.

C Walk down the left hand side of the field, cross the little ford at the end and continue up the farm track on the other side. The farm track ends at a gate. Go through and cross the field diagonally, turning right at the bottom of the field to the gate in the next corner. This brings you into Devon for a short space!

On your left is a fascinating little conglomeration of mounds, streams and trees, simply shown on the map as "Fords" and ideal for a levensies stop. You do not enter it, but skirt it by following the contour round to the left just above it.

D As soon as you have turned through a right angle, make for the hedge at the end of the field, turn right and follow this to reach the road in the corner, at E. (GR.371001)

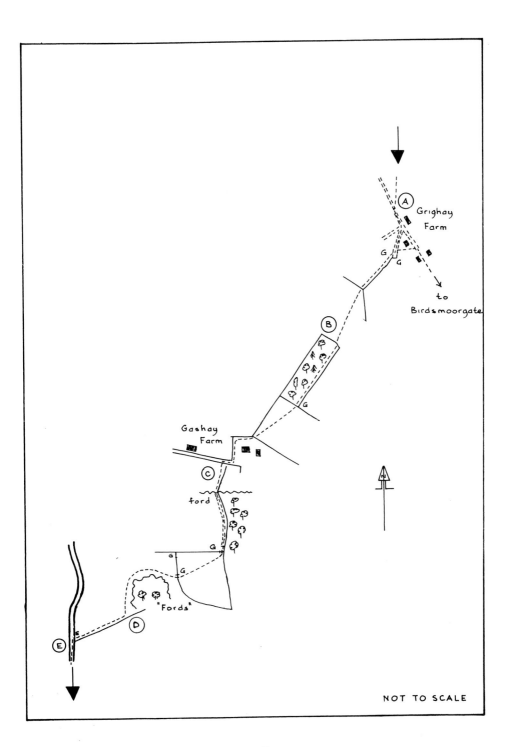

Grighay
Farm

to
Birdsmoorgate

Gashay
Farm

ford

"Fords"

NOT TO SCALE

A   Once out on the road, you turn left and follow it for about 200 yards, to a group of houses where another road comes in from behind you on the right. Keep straight on until your road curves away on your left, then leave it and continue ahead - on a little path above it - following the signpost to "Hawksmoor Farm Bungalow". A stony track leads you uphill for a quarter mile to emerge on the B3165 Axminster road and the frontier - back into Dorset.

B   Go straight across, into a minor road with a telephone kiosk on the right in its entrance and signposted to Wootton and Fishpond. About 30 yards along this road you will see a path up into the wood on your right, with a National Trust sign at its start. (GR. 372994) This will lead you up into Lamberts Castle (Note 21). Walk up, ignoring a fork to the left and keeping to the right, along a hollowed out path.

A gate at the top brings you out into the vast open space of the Castle. Walk straight ahead, aiming first at a pair of small tree clumps, and then at the top of a pylon appearing at the far end of the hill. This takes you through the earthworks of the actual fort, after which you keep along the left hand edge of the open space, leaving the Castle by the broad, green path ahead. Follow this down to the road.

C   This spot is called "Peter's Gore" from the Old English "gara" meaning a triangle of ground. History does not relate who Peter was, but the road layout here - a small rounded square with side roads going off at each corner - does look roughly triangular, or kite-shaped, on the map. If you turn right and then take the second side road to the right, you can walk along to the little hamlet of Fishpond, with its attractive little nineteenth century church.

Otherwise, take the next (i.e. third) road off the Gore, marked Whitchurch, i.e. the one which goes uphill with a pylon high above it on the left. This leads you the quarter mile up to Coney's Castle. (Note 22)

D   The Castle is entered from the National Trust car park and is well worth a visit. Walk straight through the centre and leave it by a little path down a slope at the far end. This curves down to the right and brings you to a stile out onto the road. Turn left and walk down the road for about 700 yards to a gate on your right just past the tarmac farm drive signposted to "Great Coombe Farm". (GR.372968)

E   Go through the gate, turn half left and cross the field, aiming at two trees in the hedge opposite. Over a stile and cross the second field on the same line, aiming (on a clear day) at the V-shape of Lyme Regis/Charmouth Bay on the horizon. Once through the gate into a third field, follow the same line as before. Just before the corner you go through a gate on your right and walk along the next field parallel to the hedge on your left, to a gate in the corner at F.

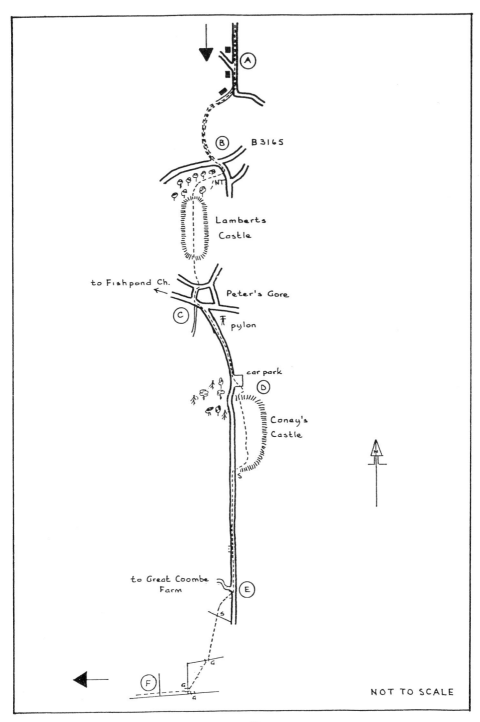

A   Continue along the left hand edge of the next field but leave it by a gate on your left just before the corner. Then walk diagonally downhill towards the buildings you can see at the bottom, where there is a stile out onto the road. This is Wootton Fitzpaine, one of the only two villages in this part of Dorset which are not on the coast.

B   Turn right and walk along the road, through the top end of the village, for about quarter of mile keeping straight on at a T-junction, along the minor road signposted Monkton Wyld and Fishpond. When the road starts to drop downhill, watch for a fire hydrant sign on your right and turn left at GR.361958 into a farm track leading to some barns. At the end of the first building, take the track on the right and follow it as it curves round to the left.

C   After about 200 yards from the barns, your track is about to drop down to a gate, but you leave it and go through the second of two gates close together on your right. Follow the hedge on your right along the top of a field and cross a dilapidated plank bridge in the corner into a second field. Again, keep along the top edge with a stone wall on your right and then turn down to a little red-roofed barn on your left. Turn right here, passing the barn on your left and continue to the stile in the next hedge. The next field is crossed diagonally left, aiming at the trees in the bottom corner.

D   This brings you to a gate in the hedge on your right. Through the gate, turn left, through a second gate, turn right and walk along parallel to a stream with the hedge on your right. Go through the next gate and cross the field on the same line, aiming towards the right hand end of the large group of trees on the far side. You should hit a spot on the bank of a tiny stream from which you can see across to a stile on the opposite bank. Ford the stream, climb to the stile and, once over it, turn left and walk a few yards to a second (and waymarked) stile. Then turn right and walk a few yards along to a third stile. Walk half right down the bank and straight on aiming at some tumbledown buildings and going through a small gate to reach them. This fascinating little spot, which must once have been a small settlement, is buried in undergrowth in the summer, but the path is always (just!) visible.

E   Pass between the first two buildings and then a third one on your left. Within a few yards your track turns right uphill at GR.351957 and you leave it and keep straight on, through the gate ahead and along the bottom edge of a field. After about 15 yards turn left, cross a concrete bridge and turn right along the stream to a gate 20 yards ahead. Then follow the wheeltracks in the grass straight ahead through two fields - gate to gate, parallel to the stream.

F   In the third field, which has a barn in it, watch out for a gate in the trees on your right, with a stream crossing behind it. When you reach it, (GR.347961) turn left and walk uphill, passing the barn on your right and aiming at the right hand hedge, and joining a cart track which leads to a gate into the next field. Go through and follow the track up to the right hand corner where there is a confluence of hedges. Be careful here because you need to take the gate in the hedge coming up from your left, first crossing a tiny ford. In this, the third field from the bottom, you walk diagonally left and go through a gate beside a large oak, with another tiny little water-course beside it.

G   Now you can see Penn Farm ahead. Cross the field aiming at a flat-roofed, corrugated barn slightly to the left of the main buildings and go through the gate between it and an oak tree. Then turn right and walk the few yards up onto the farm entrance drive. Turn left and follow the drive round until you come out onto the road at H.

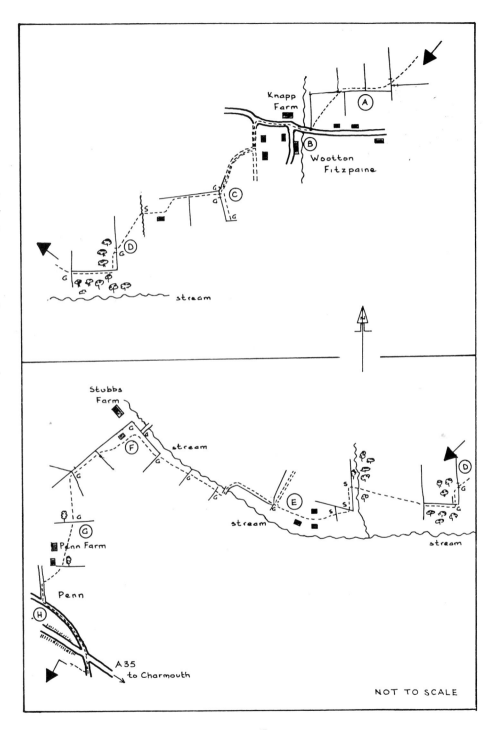

Knapp
Farm

Wootton
Fitzpaine

A

B

C

D

stream

Stubbs
Farm

F

G

D

E

H

Penn Farm

Penn

A35
to Charmouth

stream

stream

stream

NOT TO SCALE

A   You are now on a slip road off the main A35 road to Lyme Regis. Up to your right the main road splits for a dual carriageway section. To the left a minor road descends to join the A35 just below the exit from your slip road.

Turn left and walk nearly to the tip of the island between you and the main road and cross the latter. To the right of two small ash trees you should be able to walk down through the scrub and over a stile. If the scrub has overtaken the little path down the bank, turn left and walk along to the minor road. Almost immediately you will see, down to the right, a track leading back over, parallel to the side road. (GR342952) Fork back along this, through a gate and along the top edge of a field to a second gate. Go through this, turn left and walk down , with the hedge and ditch on your left, to a gate into the wood at the bottom.

Follow the path through the wood and, after about 350 yards, turn left at a footpath junction at the bottom of a rather boggy slope. After another 250 yards, you curve left into a large , stony area, with a track coming in from your right. Continue along the stony bit for a few yards and then turn left onto a path going uphill. Follow this through the wood for about ¾ of a mile, emerging through a gate, over a little ford and up a slope into the open at Rhodes Barton.

B   Walk up towards the house, swing left round its garden and then right, passing a long barn on your left. After about 200 yards you pass some barns on your left and a footpath signposted to Penn Cross. The track rises, veering gradually round to the left, passing beside an avenue of intermittent trees. Just after passing a drive down to a house on the right, go through a gate and see two pairs of centre-opening gates, one on each side of your track. (GR.339937)

C   Go through the gate on your right. Your line here is straight down the field, slightly to the right of the telegraph pole in the middle but there is a large boggy section beside it, so it is best to circle round to the right. In fact there is a clear little path round the right hand edge of the field down to the gate in the corner. Through this and down the next field - parallel but not close to the hedge on the left. From these fields you can see across the Lim Valley towards Up Lyme and Wadley Hill.

D   At the bottom there is a gate at the right hand end of a row of conifers concealing the site of the sewage works. This leads you onto a stony track with a high wire fence beside it. Follow the track round to the right, over a wide bridge (Heron Bridge) and out into the space in front of the old mill. Turn left at once at the footpath sign and walk down a little path alongside a stream. Keep straight on through two gates, the second one at the end of a footbridge. (GR.333933)

E   Once over the stile, turn left and follow a fairly clear track in the grass to the far side where you find both a kissing-gate and a stile. Down to the river - the Lim - and over the footbridge, pausing to look across to the waterfall up to the left. The little path curves to the right up the far bank and then you follow the track for about 500 yards to a road, passing a large caravan site on the left.

F   On leaving the caravan site, cross the road right-and-left into Windsor Terrace. From here you walk straight down beside the river, first on one side, then on the other, crossing the odd minor road, and into the heart of Lyme Regis (Note 23) and the end of the Wessex Ridgeway.

oooOOOooo

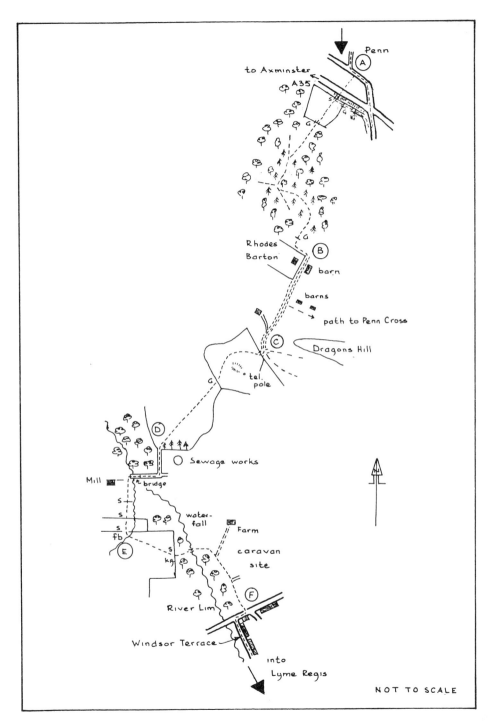

Penn

A

to Axminster

A35

s

G

G

Rhodes
Barton

B

barn

barns

path to Penn Cross

C

Dragons Hill

G

tel.
pole

D

Sewage works

Mill

bridge

s

s

s

water-
fall

Farm

fb

E

s

ka

caravan
site

F

River Lim

Windsor Terrace

into
Lyme Regis

NOT TO SCALE

PART 2
THE WALKS

Walk No. 1 - ASHMORE and THE COUNTY BOUNDARY

This 7 mile walk provides a mixture of open track and wood and, with very little effort, some splendid open views (Maps: Pathfinder 1280 (ST.81/91); Landranger 184 & 195)

A   Start from Ashmore pond (GR.913178) and follow the directions in the Wessex Ridgeway Guide as far as Stubhampton Bottom. (A, B and C on page 12)

B   Turn left along the Bottom and follow the fenced track along the valley for about half a mile, emerging onto a road on the northern outskirts of Tarrant Gunville. Walk along the left hand verge for about 120 yards and turn left up a lane signposted "Bridleway to Ashmore".

C   Having passed an attractive little house on your right and a naked new bungalow up to your left, continue along a fenced track. As you reach the end of the shady hedge behind the wire on the right you will be flabbergasted to encounter an enormous, new house on the right. Keep straight on, through a gate and past the house.

The valley widens a bit and you continue along the track, now unfenced on the left. After a couple of hundred yards, go through a gate, ignore a track running half left up to some farm buildings and keep straight on up the valley. There is no track now, and you are in Ashmore Bottom, a quiet, green place, which goes on for half a mile.

D   The Bottom ends at a wood, Elderen Row (GR.919160). Enter it through the gate and immediately turn right up a little path which winds uphill first right and then left. Although there is nothing to show you that you have left the wood, you do so after about 200 yards from the gate, and will then be walking inside a scrubby sort t of double hedge. Another 200 yards later you reach a track crossing from left to right, down a little 2 foot bank.

E   Drop down, turn right for 20 yards to a gate. Ignore this and follow the track round to the left. You will be on this for about a quarter mile, with a fence on your right over which you get a splendid view down Tollard Green Bottom to the Tarrants. Towards the end of the trees on your left, watch out in them for the remains of the Roman road which crosses your track here. It was part of a road between Bath and Bradbury Rings in Dorset, a great road junction in Roman times. The road continued down across the valley to your right, then up to the left of the tiny wood on the upslope and to the left of another wood at the end of the next field, but there is no trace of it on the ground.

Soon the path drops more steeply downhill and round to the left and continues between the fences alongside a sort of horse-gallop made of ashes. You are now in Wiltshire (GR.929163).

F   From here the path runs alongside the ash track, with the barbed wire fence between you and it on your left. The first 500 yards are inside a wood and are very overgrown, with occasional hazards in the shape of fallen trees. If not too tired, it is worth taking an occasional loop up to the right to avoid these - a carpet of cowslips in a clearing was discovered this way. The writer must admit to having occasionally slipped over the barbed wire to walk along the green verge beside the ash track in one or two places along the whole of this stretch. Even when the path does emerge from the wood and continues along a wide-fenced strip, it is very overgrown and full of hidden lumps and bumps. Representations have been made to the R.A. - Wilts Area for help in improving matters.

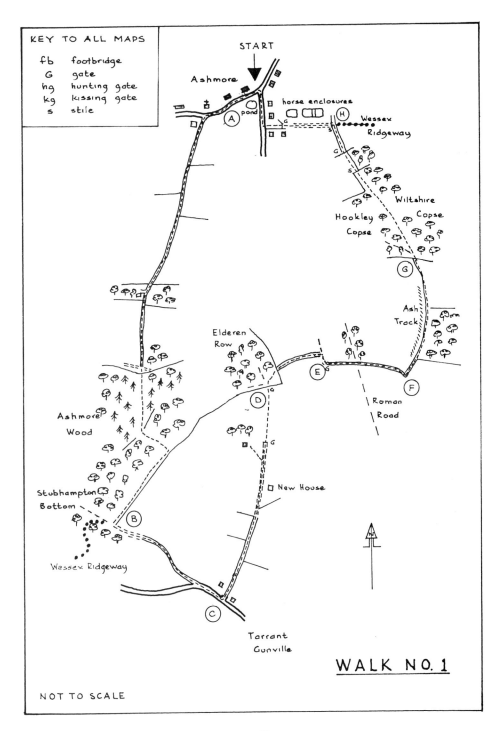

KEY TO ALL MAPS

fb footbridge
G gate
hg hunting gate
kg kissing gate
s stile

START

Ashmore

horse enclosures

Wessex Ridgeway

Wiltshire Copse

Hookley Copse

Ash Track

Elderen Row

Roman Road

Ashmore Wood

Stubhampton Bottom

Wessex Ridgeway

New House

Tarrant Gunville

WALK NO. 1

NOT TO SCALE

G   This section ends at a wood. There is a path up to the right which runs up to the road. Ignore it and keep straight on, taking the right fork after about 100 yards. You are walking along the County boundary. The wood is called Wiltshire Copse on your right and the part in Dorset on the left is Hookley Copse. It used to be a beautiful wood, green and open, and alive with bluebells and anemones in spring but has become very grown in during the last few years.

After half a mile you reach the end of the wood on your left and walk along, still just inside the trees on the right, glancing half left up the slope at the outskirts of Ashmore. Leave the wood by a stile and continue ahead with the fence on your right to enter a fenced track inside a tree belt by a hunting gate.

H   Towards the end of the tree belt there is a stile on your left and, on your right another stile giving onto a cultivated field. Here you turn left, over the stile, and are now on the Wessex Ridgeway. This insignificant spot is where the route crosses the border into Dorset (GR.917179).

Follow the wide fenced track west beside the horse enclosures on your right, through a gate beside a bungalow, and out onto the road. Turn right and walk up to Ashmore Pond.

oooOOOooo

Walk No. 2 - PIMPERNE LONG BARROW

A 7½ mile circular walk, taking in a very short stretch of the Ridgeway. Although not on the "tops" it provides a series of long, open views and the walking is easy throughout. (Maps: Pathfinder 1281 (ST.81/91); Landranger 195)

A   Start from the top of Stubhampton Down by taking the bridleway signposted "Pimperne" mentioned at E on page 12 of the Ridgeway Guide (GR.894144). There is space for a car. (Two other possible starting places are mentioned in the text at E below and at end of para G on page 54.)

The bridleway takes you south-east down the headland of a field, with a wood on your right. The headland ends at a hunting gate, after which you follow a very muddy path along the edge of the wood and out through a tree belt at the end, into a field. Walk straight across this, lining up on the right hand telegraph pole in the centre, and out onto a farm road. Cross this and enter a double-fenced track arrowed "bridleway" and follow it for about a quarter mile.

B   Keep right at a rather attractive little tree-filled hollow on your right, and continue along the fenced and hedged track. You will now be following this SSE for about a mile, first passing on your right a wood called Harbins Park (GR.904135). This was one of the enclosures formed by landowners in Norman times for the purpose of collecting deer for fresh meat. They were enclosed by earth banks with a ditch behind, called "park-pales" which allowed the deer to leap in but prevented them from getting out again.

Harbins Park is one of the best preserved. It comprises 115 acres and you will obtain occasional glimpses of its eastern pale as you walk down beside it. As can be imagined, such parks were not popular with the lords of Cranborne Chase and there was a famous law suit over this one in the 16th century.

C   Towards the end of Harbins Park a farm track goes off to the left but you step right and left and keep straight on, then over a minor road and past another two fields. Here the grass track broadens, passing Pimperne Wood on the left. This section is very attractive and full of wild flowers and birds.

D   After leaving Pimperne Wood, the track drops down into a little valley, with some farm buildings away to the right. However, you keep straight on, uphill again, along the left hand edge of three fields. As you enter the fourth field you find yourself on a hedged and fenced track. Follow this for about 200 yards to a T junction with a metalled farm road and a barn on your left.
(N.B. If you are staying in the Blandford area, you could start this walk from Pimperne at the west end of this concrete road. Park at GR.906097 at the end of the road running uphill from the church, past the shop, and walk straight along, due NE, until you reach the barn.)

E   Turn left, passing the barn on your left and water tower on your right and follow a narrow, fenced and rather overgrown path for 300 yards to a gate. Through this and you emerge onto the cross-piece of a T junction with Pimperene Long Barrow in front of you (GR.917105). This neolithic barrow is described by Jacquetta Hawkes as "perhaps the finest earthen long barrow in the whole country". It is 106 metres long and 27 metres wide with its widest and highest end to the south, and ditches along each side. It has never been excavated. Access to it can be gained by a stile in its fence.

F   Turn left into a green drove, passing the barrow on your right and go through the metal hunting gate into a vast field. Cross this diagonally right aiming at a gate on the far side. If you cannot see this, aim towards the right hand end of a wood which runs from quarter left to half right ahead of you. In the next field follow the track ahead with the fence on your left to another gate.

G   Here, ignore the track as it turns right and keep straight on, with the wood on your left. Halfway along you enter a fenced track and, once past the wood, keep the same line for a quarter mile, first between fields, and then edging a tree belt to your right, for about 600 yards and then passing some houses on the right. When your track ends at a T-junction with a road, turn right and walk along the road for about half a mile. Approximately 250 yards after passing a road coming in from the left, you will spot a signposted stile on your left, in a gap between the hedge and some conifers. You can identify it because there is a kissing-gate on the other side of the road. This leads to a little path to the church. This is Tarrant Gunville and, if hungry and thirsty, you are only 250 yards from the Bugle Horn Inn. To reach this, continue down the road for 100 yards, turn right at the T-junction and walk another 100 yards to find it on your right.

(N.B. This would be another good starting point for the circular walk, leaving you car at the Bugle Horn at GR.927127 with the landlord's permission.)

H   If not digressing to the pub, negotiate the stile and walk straight ahead with the hedge on your right. From here you will be walking due NW for a mile and a quarter across fields - gate to gate (sometimes stile to stile) keeping always along the lower, right hand edge of the fields. The village of Tarrant Gunville is strung out along the valley just below you to the right.

J   About halfway along, after dropping downhill along the edge of a cultivated field, a bridleway comes in from your left and here you go through the gate at its end - on your right - which brings you out into a sort of yard full of concrete pig houses (GR.919135). Turn left, passing the first one on your left and look for a stile, slightly above you in the hedge ahead and behind a small grey hutch about 5 feet high. Negotiate this stile and then walk straight on, with the hedge on your right.

The next gate is down in the bottom corner of the field and, once through it, you have to do a left/ right, following a clearly defined track along the contour. The gate at the end of this field brings you out slightly uphill and here you should turn right and then left to follow the valley along the bottom. Just before you reach a white cottage on your right, turn uphill following the edge of a wood on your right until you reach a stile into this - in an angle of the wood. Follow a barely discernible little path straight through the wood, leaving it by a second stile. Then turn right and walk downhill to the road.

K   On reaching the road turn right and walk about 50 yards downhill. At the bottom the road veers round to the right and you can see a signpost pointing hard left back along the valley. Turn left here and follow the track NW for three quarters of a mile until you see the beginning of a wood coming down on your right.

L   You are now in Stubhampton Bottom and back on the Wessex Ridgeway. Follow the directions at D on page 12 of the main guide, back to where you started.

oooOOOooo

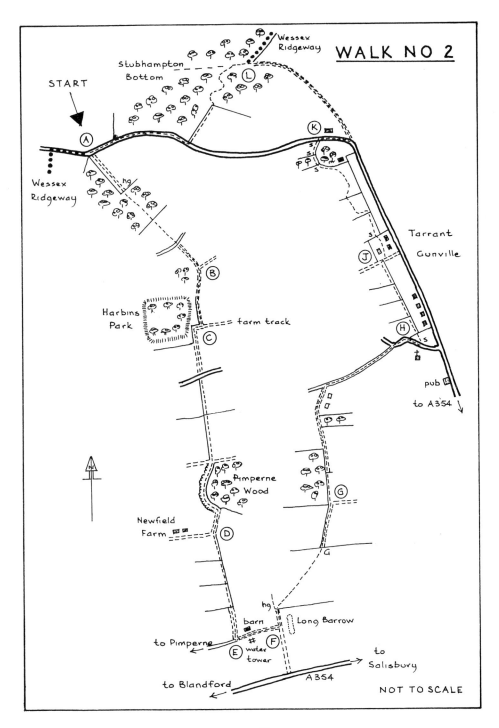

WALK NO 2

Wessex Ridgeway

Stubhampton Bottom

START

L

K

Tarrant Gunville

A

Wessex Ridgeway

hg

J

H

Harbins Park

B

farm track

C

pub

to A354

Pimperne Wood

G

Newfield Farm

D

G

hg

barn

Long Barrow

to Pimperne

E

water tower

F

to Salisbury

to Blandford

A354

NOT TO SCALE

Walk No. 3 - WINTERBORNE STICKLAND

This 9 mile walk only takes in a very short section of the Wessex Ridgeway. It leads you above the Winterborne Valley - down one side with a splendid view gradually opening up to the south, and up the other, through fields and woodland. (Maps: Pathfinder 1300 (ST.80/90; Landranger sheet 194)

A   Start from the picnic site/car park at the top of Okeford Hill (GR. 813093). This is on the road running north/south between Okeford Fitzpaine and Tunworth, and is about half a mile south of the former.

   Leave the car park by the stile in the far corner and follow the lane running uphill. After about three quarters of a mile you will see a NT sign on your left, beside a gate. Turn through it, skirt the pond and over the stile into the Ringmoor Settlement (Note 6).

B   Walk along the top edge of the site for about 600 yards until you see a hunting gate on your right. Go through and cross the field diagonally left. This brings you to the top of a track through some trees and then running downhill - still on the same line as the field crossing - but now with a hard surface. Down below you are cottages and buildings, once part of the Turnworth House estate. The house, Thomas Hardy's model for Hintock House in "The Woodlanders" has been demolished since the war.

   When you reach the bottom of the slope, turn left and walk a few yards along the farm road to the last building on the right. Just past this, turn and walk diagonally up the slope to your right, keeping more or less the same line as the one you followed downhill. There is a stile in the hedge at the top and once over this, cross the next field on the same line, touching the tree clump to your left, to another stile. Keeping the same line, cut the corner of the third field and cross to a gap in the hedge on your right.

   The true line of the path here is diagonally across the field below but, as there is a good headland down its right hand side which takes you where you want to go, and as the filed is usually cultivated, nobody minds your taking a short cut. So walk down the right hand headland straight across the track at the bottom and up the other side to a glorious clump of beeches. Then keep straight on along the clearly defined track. Follow this as it curves round to the right after about 350 yards and walk to the gate at the far end. Go through this and walk straight downhill and through the hunting gate at the bottom (into the mud!) (GR.817069).

   On the other side of the farm road running along the valley, is another hunting gate. Go through this and walk up the very steep hill, with a fence on your left, to a third hunting gate at the top.

C   Keep straight on, this time with a fence on your right. When this leaves you to go off to the right, keep your line, walking between two cultivated areas, first topping the rise, then dropping slowly downhill. Part way down the slope you hit a farm track running left to right across your route. A waymarked post directs you to the right. Do this and keep along the track for nearly a quarter mile, where the track turns right uphill.

D   At this point you turn left (at another waymarked post) and follow a wide, uncultivated strip down to the trees at the bottom. Keeping line, go through the gateway in the scrubby hedge and walk uphill, with fence and wood on your right, aiming at a solitary tree on the skyline. This brings you out onto the road (GR.818057).

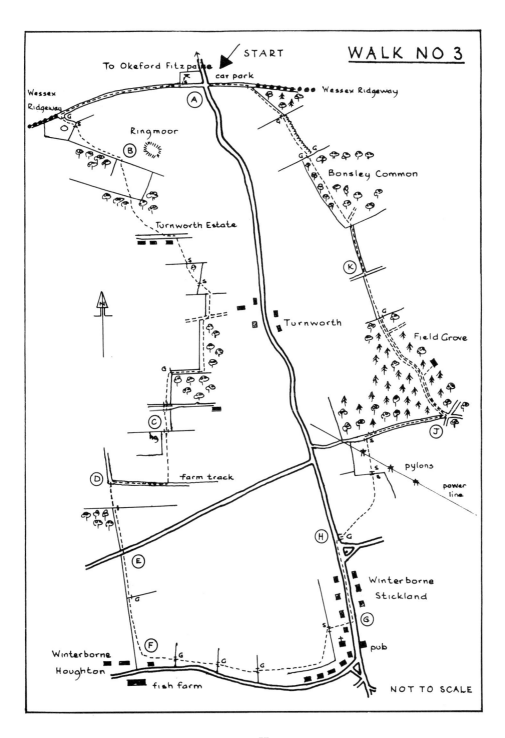

WALK NO 3

START

To Okeford Fitzpaine

car park

Wessex Ridgeway

Wessex Ridgeway

Ringmoor

Bonsley Common

Turnworth Estate

Turnworth

Field Grove

farm track

pylons

power line

Winterborne Stickland

Winterborne Houghton

pub

fish farm

NOT TO SCALE

A B C D E F G H J K

E   On the opposite side, go through the hunting gate and walk straight downhill, keeping the hedges of two fields on your right, until you are very nearly at the road at the bottom.

F   Here turn left and follow the contour round behind the little house, gate to gate, parallel with the road, until you can see into the corner of the last field. Here you cut the corner, passing under an electricity line and following a clearly defined, narrow path, ending at a stile at the top of a bank. Negotiate this and follow the stony lane down to the road.

G   This is the main street of Winterborne Stickland and, if thirsty, you will find The Crown about 100 yards down to the right. Dorset has a number of villages with "Winterborne" in their name, called after streams which only run in the winter when the chalk becomes saturated. You will not see the stream in the part of the village the walk takes you through but it is worth strolling on past the pub for a short distance to the pretty little corner by the school where this particular Winterborne becomes visible and where you can see the village sign (GR.835045). Designed and made by local craftsmen, this was unveiled by the sculptress, Dame Elizabeth Frink in 1988. An information leaflet can be obtained at the Post Office.

Otherwise, turn left on leaving the footpath and walk up the village to its far end, continuing for about 80 yards past a small green and a huge chestnut tree at a right turn.

H   Turn into the first gate on your right and walk diagonally left up the field. When you see a pair of pylons on the skyline, aim to the right of the left-hand one. Keep your line until the trees behind the pylons come into view and then watch for a stile in the hedge ahead. Over this, and its mate on the other side, and walk ahead to a point about 5 yards to the right of the pylon nearest to you. From here you should be able to see the stile in the far hedge, against the trees beyond. Over this, turn right and follow the track along the edge of the wood for about a quarter of a mile to a big junction (GR.841064).

J   Take the wide, stony track going off to the left and follow it for nearly a mile through the wood (Field Grove) leaving it for a grassy track in order to maintain direction for the last 200 yards. A gate at the far end of the wood brings you out into a field where you continue straight ahead along the left hand edge and out onto a lane.

K   Here you walk straight ahead, along a double hedged track, and enter the wood at the end. This is called Bonsley Common and is far more attractive than Field Grove. Maintaining direction you follow the clear track through to the far end - about 800 yards - and when you emerge into a field sloping down to your left, you keep straight on along the top, with the hedge on your right for half a mile. This is Turnworth Down and you are looking across to Ringmoor near where the walk started.

At the end of the second field a gate brings you our onto the stony lane on the Ridgeway route. Turn left and walk down to the road and across to the car park/picnic site where your started.

oooOOOooo

Walk No. 4 - ANSTY AND BINGHAMS MELCOMBE

This is a 5 mile panhandle-shaped walk from the Ridgeway and back, the first mile and a half being over the same ground in opposite directions. Alternatively Ridgeway walkers can use it just to walk down the 1½ miles to the Fox Inn at Ansty for refreshment and return the same way. (Maps: Pathfinder 1299 (ST.60/70); Landranger 194)

A   Park on waste ground at junction of roads down to Woolland and Stoke Wake on Bulbarrow Hill (GR. 773059). Take the road signposted "Stoke Wake and Mappowder" watching for your first site of Rawlesbury Camp ahead (Note 7). When you see a gate in the fence on your left, go through and follow a green track into the camp.

Having enjoyed the view from the remains of the old wooden cross on a mound, leave the camp by the little path on the lower rampart below the cross. Follow this through a hunting gate in the trees and right round to the other side of the camp. Here keep a small wood to your right and walk down to the gate ahead. Follow the same line steeply down the next field to another gate.

B   Here you leave the Ridgeway (GR.76400555). Do not go through the gate but turn left and walk downhill - not alongside the hedge but slightly to the left of it where a faintly discernible track leads you down to the right of a dilapidated corrugated iron building. This is all that remains of the Old Rawlesbury Farm still shown on the map.

Go through the gateway down ahead between some tall trees and walk down to the bottom left hand corner of the field where you can see a gate between a tree belt to its left and a small wood to its right. As you approach the gate you can see the lane ahead going uphill, and at the top of the rise, the new buildings of what is now Rawlesbury Farm. (On your return journey be careful to take the left hand of the two gates at this point. Also do not follow the tempting cart track running quarter left uphill but stay parallel to the right hand fence.)

Once through the gate, cross a very muddy bridge with a small pond down to its left. This pond was made by the farmer a year or two ago from a spot which was always very muddy and wet and there are already some interesting plants growing up in it.

After the bridge you continue up the, now stony and muddy, track, fenced on both sides, and walk straight through the farmyard at the top. (On your return journey along this stretch, do not fail to look to your right at the beautiful curving valley below Bulbarrow, nor at the stunning sight of Rawlesbury Camp quarter right ahead.) Continue along the now made-up lane as it curves round to the left. Ignore a tempting right turn at a house called White Thorns and follow the lane to a T-junction. You are now a the beginning of Ansty (Note 25).

C   Turn right here and walk to the road at the end of the lane. Keep straight along this for about 200 yards.

D   Just past a very handsome property on the left, once called Moonfleet, now holiday flats (GR.767040), turn through the gate on the left and walk straight along the top of the field, with the old farm buildings on your left, and go through into the next field. Look straight across to the far hedge and aim at a single, umbrella-shaped tree in it. This will take you along a wide green pathway across a rather boggy bit at the bottom of the dip ahead. Emerging from this you should be able to see up to the stile roughly quarter right ahead. On the other side of the stile a bridleway crosses from left to right but you keep straight on. Before doing so, have a look at the view. Nettlecombe Tout is over to your right and between it and you is the Dorsetshire Gap (Note 8) which is on the next lap of the Ridgeway. The hill diagonally right ahead is Henning Hill and the valley down to your right is that of the Mash Water, along which you will soon be walking.

Continue walking along the top (left hand edge) of the field (shown as two on the O.S. map but now amalgamated into one) and out onto the road at the far end.

E   The rather pleasant Victorian house on the left was Chilmore. Turn right and walk 400 yards down to the Fox Inn (GR.766033).

F   On leaving the Fox you can either return to the Ridgeway the way you came or turn left and walk on down the road. 200 yards after passing a left turn, the road dips to a bridge (over the Mash Water) and about 50 feet after this you will spot two stiles on your left. Take the right hand one and walk straight ahead through the scrub, taking the first opportunity you can make your way down to the left hand fence. Follow this to the corner, go over the bar stile ahead, then over the second of two stiles half left and then turn right and walk along with the fence on your right. This takes you along a rather attractive little valley with a number of large oak trees bordering your path.

Pass a field corner going off to your right, keep your line, pass between another oak and a fence corner on the left, just above the water and continue along the top of the bank with the Water down to your left.

Next you come to a pair of stiles with a footbridge between them. Once over these you remain at the top of the slope which runs down to the water and walk up the edge of the field towards a gate at the top. Once through this you keep to the same line, above the stream, but now there is a hedge on your left. This brings you to a stile after which you go downhill and up again to a gate which leads out onto a wide, grass strip. Turn right and walk down this.

G   You are now walking down beside the manor house of Binghams Melcombe (Note 26) of which you can obtain an occasional glimpse over the wall on your left. Notice also the enormous yew hedge. At the bottom of the grass strip, keep straight on along the drive and follow this round to the left, passing the entrance to the manor. Keep straight on, passing the little church of St. Andrew on your right, and cross the Devils Brook by a very splendid footbridge. Turn left and walk up the field, making for the gate in the top right hand corner. This brings you out onto the corner of a road. Do not turn left but keep straight on along the road for about 80 yards. When it veers right, leave it and turn left up a lane. Follow the lane uphill for about half a mile, watching for the start of a wood on your left (GR.776028).

H   At the top corner of this wood, turn onto a track on the left which follows the top edge of the wood downhill. At the end, leave the definitive line which goes diagonally down across the field, and follow local custom by continuing along the track, between fences, where it runs between two fields to emerge into a third. All along this last bit you have a splendid view down to Aller and the man-made lakes at the bottom of the hill. At the end of the fenced track, go into the next field, turn left and walk down it, with the hedge on your left.

J   Do not go out through the gate at the bottom of the field (unless visiting Ivy Cottage which you will find straight along the road) but turn right at it and follow the bottom edge of the field. Continue round to the right with a fence on your left until this turns into a corner with a stile leading down to a footbridge. Cross here, over the second stile and then diagonally right through a new plantation to a third stile. Then walk straight across, through the tall reedy area, to the far hedge where a plank bridge takes you across a ditch and over a stile to the next field. Walk up the next two fields with the hedge on your right, negotiating a stile between them, and out onto the road at E.

You are now back at Chilmore and are facing the gate at which you emerged before visiting the Fox. Return to the Ridgeway by the way you came.

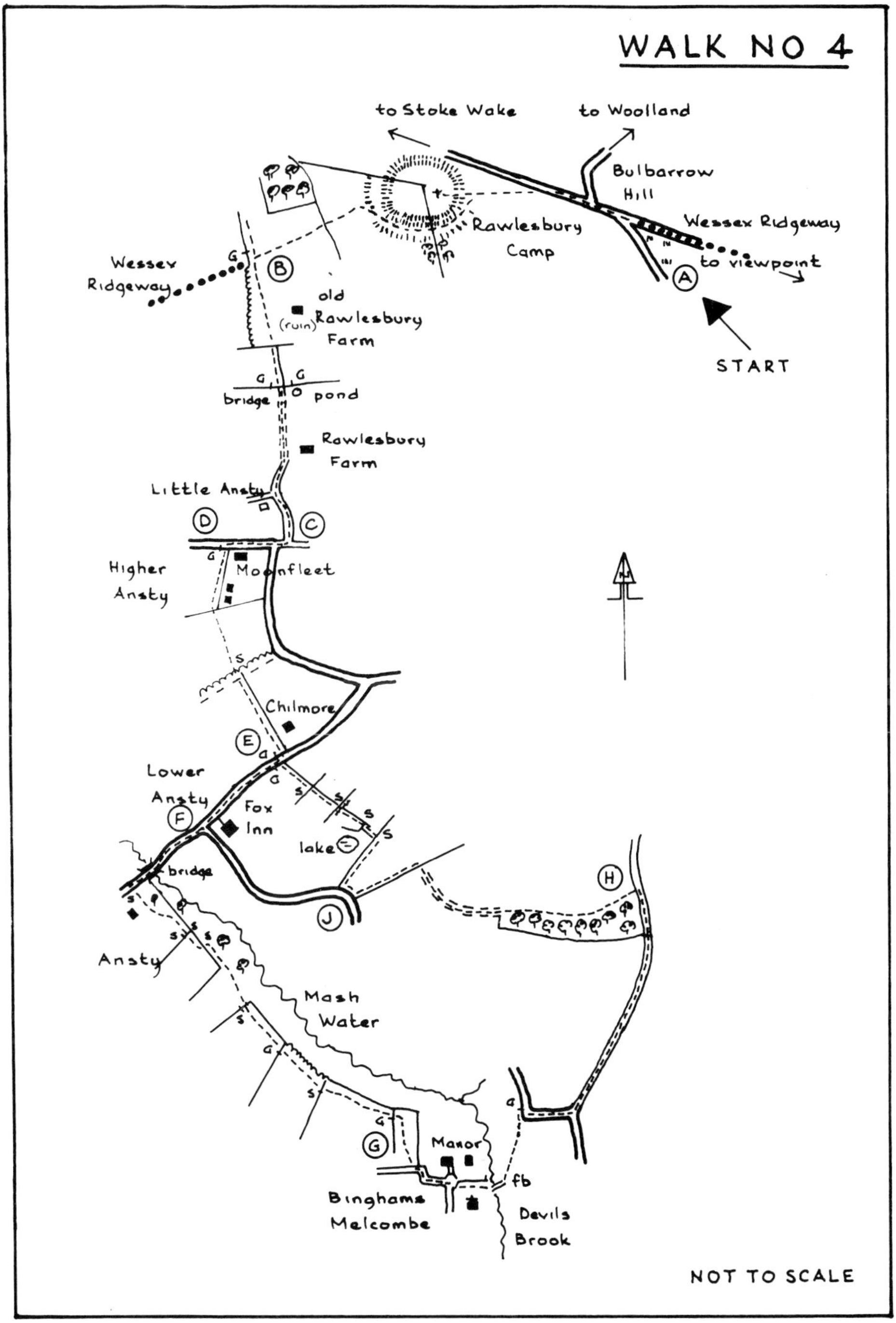

WALK NO 4

to Stoke Wake

to Woolland

Bulbarrow Hill

Wessex Ridgeway

Rawlesbury Camp

to viewpoint

Ⓐ

START

Wessex Ridgeway

Ⓑ

old (ruin) Rawlesbury Farm

bridge pond

Rawlesbury Farm

Little Ansty

Ⓓ Ⓒ

Moonfleet

Higher Ansty

Chilmore

Ⓔ

Lower Ansty

Ⓕ Fox Inn

lake

Ⓙ

Ⓗ

bridge

Ansty

Mash Water

Ⓖ Manor

Binghams Melcombe

fb

Devils Brook

NOT TO SCALE

61

Walk No. 5 - MILTON ABBAS

This 7½ mile circuit can be used as a way of getting off the Ridgeway to see Milton Abbey and Milton Abbas (Note 24) and for rest and refreshment, or as a pleasant walk in its own right with spectacular views on the return journey. (Maps: Pathfinder 1299 and 1300 (ST.60/70 & 80/90); Landranger 194)

A   Start from the viewpoint at Delcombe Head (GR. 783059). This is on Bulbarrow Hill, at point D on page 18 of the Ridgeway Guide. Turn left along the road in front of the car park. After a few yards, take the left fork signposted "Ansty and Hilton" and continue for about 400 yards to the end of the wood on the left.

B   Turn left down the drive to Bulbarrow Farm - signposted 'Bridleway to Hilton & Milton Abbey'. Pass the entrance to the old Nissen huts on the left, ignore a green left fork soon after, and follow the farm road straight ahead for a quarter mile - with a wood on the left and a thin belt of trees on the right. At the end of the wood there is a track crossroad with a barn on the right and a red brick house over to the left. Keep straight on, through a gate and along a double hedged, then double fenced, track. You are looking down at Delcombe Bottom to your left and the attractive group of buildings half left across it is Delcombe Manor.

At the end of the track there is another barn on the right. Fork left and go through the gate into a long field. Walk along the top of this and the next one, keeping the hedge on your right. At the end of the second field go through the gate into the Green Hill Down Nature Reserve and continue along the top edge as before. The Reserve is a private one created by a well known local farmer.

C   Watch out for a stile and gate in the hedge on your right (GR.789038) as you will be turning through there on your return journey, but keep straight on now. On leaving the Reserve by another gate, continue in the same direction - steeply downhill - for half a mile, along a very narrow little path winding down to the road. As you near the bottom, look half left across the valley and you will get a splendid view of Milton Abbey. Then turn left and walk along the road for about 300 yards and take the second turn off to the right (GR.758027).

D   This is a drive entrance to Milton Abbey School. Turn into it, ignoring a notice on one of the stone pillars which says "Private Road. No public entry to church or house. No horses." The school is quite happy for members of the public to walk down this drive. If the Abbey itself is not open to visitors, there will be a notice here "Abbey Closed Today". At the end of the drive, keep straight on past the school buildings and then do a right/left which brings you past the main entrance to the Abbey. It is normally open to the public without charge but please leave a donation.

Keep straight on along the west face of the Abbey and then onto a gravelly path curving downhill to the left, with some tennis courts below to the right. Cross a drive and follow the path for another quarter mile, beside a series of lakes and islands, until it emerges onto the road at a small lodge.

E   Turn left onto the road and follow it round to the left and up the centre of Milton Abbas to the Hambro Arms at F. Return by the same route as far as the stile and gate in the Green Hill Down Nature Reserve at C, then turn left through the gate and follow the track for 200 yards to the first gate on your right.

G   Go through the gate and walk up the mile to the road, field to field, keeping the hedge to your right and entering a double-hedged track for the last quarter mile. This stretch is known as Ice Drove and it affords some splendid views to the west.

H   On emerging onto the road, turn right and walk the half mile back to the viewpoint.

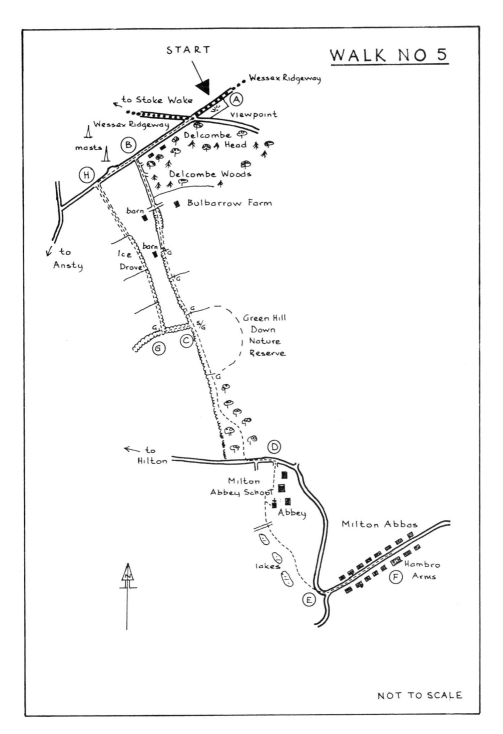

START

WALK NO 5

Wessex Ridgeway

to Stoke Wake

(A)

viewpoint

Wessex Ridgeway

masts

(B)

Delcombe Head

(H)

Delcombe Woods

barn

Bulbarrow Farm

to
Ansty

barn

Ice
Drove

G

G

G

S/G

Green Hill
Down
Nature
Reserve

(G)

(C)

G

to
Hilton

(D)

Milton
Abbey School

Abbey

Milton Abbas

lakes

Hambro
Arms

(F)

(E)

NOT TO SCALE

Walk No. 6 - LYSCOMBE HILL AND HOG HILL

A 6 or 7 mile circuit comprising two splendid ridges and one little hidden valley, with a one-mile optional digression to one of the Wessex Ridgeway's beauty spots - the Dorsetshire Gap (Note 8). (Maps: Pathfinder 1299 (ST.60/70) & 1318 (SY.69/79); Landranger 194)

A   Start at the Folly lane crossing on the Mappowder/Piddletrenthide road (GR.728032). It is 2 miles south of Mappowder and you will recognise it by a sign on the east corner saying "Folly Farmhouse".
Walk up the lane to the east, past the farmhouse. After about a quarter mile, shortly after leaving a wooded section, fork right through a gate and follow the green track diagonally along and up the side of the hill. At the top go through a gate on your left at the beginning of a small wood and walk down the field keeping the wood, then a hedge and then another small wood, on your right.

B   At the end of the field, a gate brings you onto a rather attractive little spot, with a cross-dyke going of to the left and some beautiful beech trees. Continue down the next field until you reach a massive pig farm on the right. The next few yards may be a bit overgrown, but stick close to the hedge on your right, then through a hunting gate and out onto a made-up road. This is the service road to the pig farm. Turn left along it and follow it for a half a mile down to a road, passing a dreary waste on the right which was once part of Thorncombe farm - now a small factory.

C   Cross the road and walk down the headland of a very long field with the hedge on your left. Go through the gate at the bottom and, leaving the hedge, walk straight across the first 80 yards of the next field until you hit a broad green track left to right along the valley (GR.735995). Turn left onto this and follow it alongside a belt of scrub. This gives way to a rather special, thick parish boundary hedge which you keep on your left until it comes to an end.

D   Here you turn hard left to go uphill again, along a green hedged lane. Follow this round slightly right, over a very muddy ford, and on up the hill for half a mile. Pass a barn on your right, noticing the new plantation adjoining it. Go through a Hampshire gate onto a stony lane and walk up to a road.

E   Cross the road left/right and continue up the tarmac farm road signposted to Nettlecombe Farm. The tarmac goes on for half a mile to the farm. Stay on it, passing farm buildings on both sides, and then straight on, through two gates, and onto a dirt track along the top edge of a downland field with the hedge on your right. Notice the very faint signs of an ancient settlement on the left and, as you reach the next gate you will be able to see the cross-dyke up ahead and slightly to the left. After going through this gate you will have a rather intriguing earthwork covered with small trees down to your right for about a quarter mile.
At the end of the tree belt keep straight on with a fence on your right until you spot a water tower. Walk to it (GR.738029).

F   From here you can EITHER follow the Wessex Ridgeway directions back to your car at Folly, picking up at F in penultimate paragraph on page 20.

OR you can take the one-mile digression to the Gap and back. In this case, turn hard right at the water tower and walk across the field until you spot the hunting gate down on the opposite side. Go through this and walk down the green track ahead and through a gate. Follow the track downhill for about 300 yards, then turn hard back left at the fork. This brings you into the Gap.

Having signed the book, leave by the alternative route described at E on page 20 and follow the ensuing directions down to Folly.

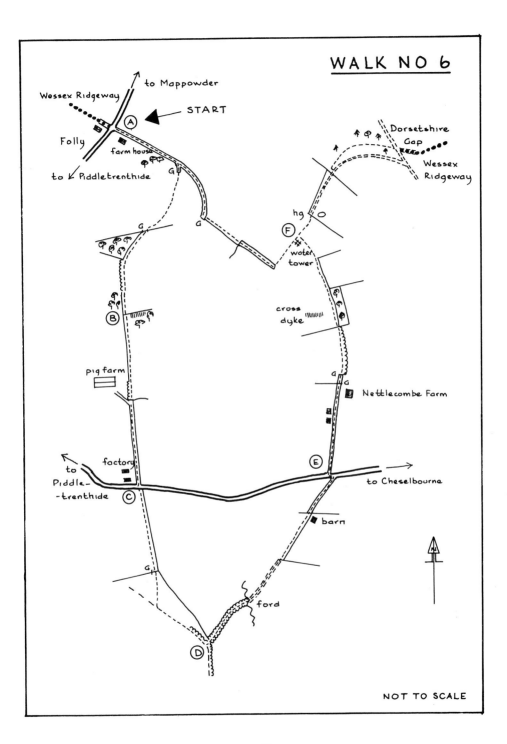

WALK NO 6

to Mappowder

Wessex Ridgeway

START

Folly

to Piddletrenthide

farm house

A

G

G

G

Dorsetshire Gap

Wessex Ridgeway

hg

F

water tower

cross dyke

B

pig farm

Nettlecombe Farm

factory

to Piddle- -trenthide

C

E

to Cheselbourne

barn

G

ford

D

NOT TO SCALE

Walk No. 7 - GORE HILL

A 7 mile circuit over two ridges and along two valleys, with a series of different and spectacular views. (Maps: Pathfinder 1299 (ST.60/70); Landranger 194)

A   Start from the south-west corner of the picnic site on Hillfield Hill, above Batcombe (GR.636039). Driving south along the A352 from Sherborne, take the second right turn after Lyons gate, signposted to Evershot. The picnic site is on the right, about a mile along the top of the ridge and you want its farthest entrance, next to the right turn down to Hillfield and Batcombe.

Leave the picnic site, cross the road and walk down the lane opposite. Continue along it as it narrows to a rather muddy little path, to join a stony lane coming in from half-right behind. Follow this in the same direction for half a mile, ignoring a left fork 100 yards later, keeping an eye on the view down to your right. You are walking along Redpost Hill above the Upper Sydling valley and can now see Row Hill, behind your right shoulder, East and Cross Hills over to the right, and Wardour Hill behind them. You have been on the Wessex Ridgeway route since joined by the stony lane, but you will be leaving it at B below.

B   After half a mile, at GR.642024, turn right along a fenced track for 200 yards with the wood of Balls Hill to your left, and then follow the track when it turns left and brings you the mile down to the valley and the road along it. Turn right and walk up the lane to Up Sydling.

C   Up Sydling is no more than a farm settlement, once occupied by a family in two farmhouses, with ancillary buildings and labourers cottages, but now taken over and gentrified. Follow the lane round to the left, past a pretentious pair of gateposts and continue for about 300 yards. Then take the right turn uphill, and follow the track as it curves left and right round Cross Hill. Keeping the fence on your left, follow the track for half a mile rising slowly, with Fishers Bottom down to your right.

Pass on your left a romantic little circle of trees with an old pond in the middle (GR.612023) and follow the fence up to the hedge at the top. Turn right here and walk along the hedge until it gives onto a farm track. Continue along this to the road.

D   Walk straight ahead up the road until it ends in a junction. Keep your line by going straight across to the gate in front of you and entering a large field. Do not cross to the visible gate ahead, but slightly to the left, aiming at two tiny spaced treetops on the skyline, until you spot the gateway on the far side. Make for this and walk along the next field with the hedge on your right. The next gate brings you into a double-hedged track. You will be following this for a quarter of a mile, dropping first gradually, then more steeply.

E   After your quarter mile, the track curves slightly right, then left, and the scrubby trees on the right end at a small, steep field (GR.610047). Enter this through a pair of tied metal gates and walk down to the gate into the next field. Continue down this, keeping as close as possible to the hedge on the left when you encounter the boggy sections lower down.

At the bottom of the field, go through a gate on the left and turn right along a lane, through a yard to pass Dyers Farm on your right, and on out onto the road. Turn right and walk up the road to Batcombe, taking first a left and then a right turn to continue uphill.

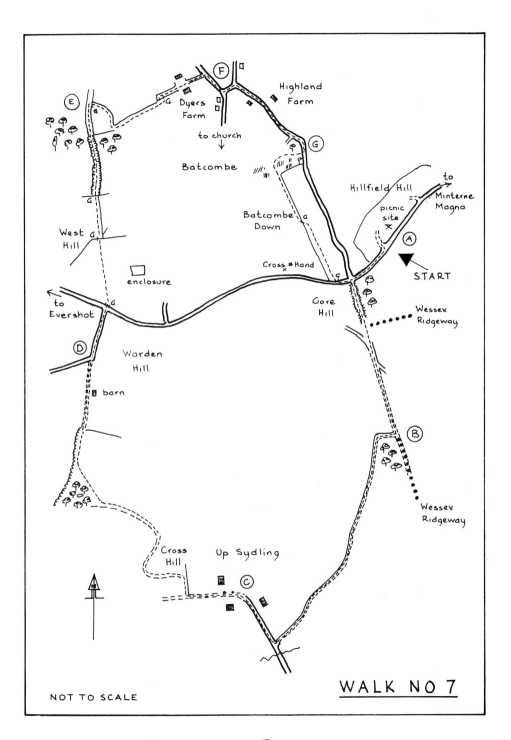

E

F   Dyers Farm

Highland Farm

Batcombe

to church

Batcombe Down

G

Hillfield Hill

picnic site

to Minterne Magna

A

START

West Hill

enclosure

Cross Hand

Gore Hill

Wessex Ridgeway

to Evershot

D

Warden Hill

barn

B

Wessex Ridgeway

Cross Hill

Up Sydling

C

NOT TO SCALE

WALK NO 7

F   Batombe itself is a small, straggly hamlet, remarkable mainly for its fifteenth century church. A seventeenth century squire, "Conjuror Minterne" - believed locally to be a white witch - is said to have tried to jump the tower on his horse from East Hill to the south and knocked one of the pinnacles off the tower.

To visit the church, do not take the left and right turns but keep straight on up the road for half a mile, returning the same way to renew the walk.

About a quarter mile after passing Highland Farm on your left, the road steepens and curves slightly left, then right. Be careful here because there is a tempting track going off to the right before the right hand curve. Ignore this and enter the next one, about 100 yards later at GR.623047.

G   The (very muddy) track leads you round the base of a series of earthworks rising high above to your left. Follow these round until you spot a narrow track going up to the left between them. Turn up this, leaving what looks like the highest point up to your left, and emerge onto a green track leading out of the earthworks. Keep your line along the ridge with a fence on your left, but watch out for a waymarked gate which takes you through to the next field to continue in the same direction but with the fence now on your right. This is Batcombe Down and at the end of the second field you will emerge on to the road next to the turning to Hillfield, with the Picnic Site a few yards past it on the left.

However, before turning back to your car, Hardy enthusiasts may care to walk along the road to the right for 250 yards to inspect the Cross and Hand which Alec D'Urberville conned Tess into believing was once a holy cross and on which he made her swear never to tempt him again. It is a small stone pillar about 3 feet high on the north side of the road at GR.632038, and was probably a Saxon boundary marker. The origin of its name is not known, but one legend has it that the carving on its top once represented a hand-held bowl intended to receive alms for poor wayfarers. Certainly the road along this spectacular ridge was once part of the Great Ridgeway route.

Walk No. 8 - THE SYDLING VALLEY AND SOME HILLS

A 7½ mile circuit taking in 1½ miles of the Ridgeway, some pleasant stretches along the Sydling Water and a glorious 2½ miles along a ridge above the Cerne and Sydling valleys. (Maps: Pathfinder 1318 (SY.69/79); Landranger Sheet 194)

A   Start from Sydling St Nicholas Church. You can park a car at the top of the lane leading to it (GR.631993). For Sydling St Nicholas, see Note 18.

Go through the white gate with a kissing-gate beside it, signposted to the church. As you enter the churchyard you will see a narrow track through the grass on your left, leading to a stile. Walk down this, over the stile and turn left through a gate and down to the right to a gate onto a hedged lane running south. Follow the lane to a rather beautiful Elizabethan stone and flint barn on your right at GR.631992. After inspecting this, continue down the lane for 300 yards to a left turn. The lane continues, curving slightly right, but you turn left and walk up to the road. Turn right.

B   About 80 yards along you will see on your left a bridleway signposted to High Street, Godmanstone and Charminster. Turn up the tarmac drive, passing a pair of little grey houses on your right. Just past them is a white sign pointing left to "sawmill" and right to Huish. Turn right here, through a white gate, and walk up towards the farm buildings, passing the very attractive Huish Farm house on your left. When you reach the large barn on your left follow the lane round to the right and continue along it through much mud, for about 400 yards.

When you reach a single storey farm building with a red corrugated roof on your left, the lane forks and you take the left fork going uphill. This takes you upwards for about a quarter mile, on a stony and rather slippery surface - hedge on right, fence on left, to the top of Shearplace Hill.

C   At the top you go through a wide gateway and turn right onto another track. Before you do so, look over the gate on the left to some rough ground with some interesting little lumps and bumps on it. This is an ancient village settlement, dated somewhere between 1360 and 1000 BC. Excavations yielded pottery, flint scrapers and a decorated bone weaving comb (GR.640986).

Having turned right, walk along the top of a field, hedge on your right, through a gate with a corrugated iron covering and continue straight ahead, passing Huish barn on your right, and through another gate. About 300 yards past the barn, the farm track does a left and right into the next field, but you leave it and go over the bar stile in front of you. Then turn half right and look down across the next field. Just beyond the clump of bushes in the middle of the field you should be able to spot a gap in the hedge on the far site. Make your way diagonally down the field and go through the gap. Turn right and walk down with the hedge on your right, following the headland round to the left and continuing through this and the next field with the hedge on your right. At the end of the second field the headland brings you to the top of a stony lane with a wood up to your left. Walk down the lane, past Magiston Farm and out onto the road at D. Turn left and walk down the road for about half a mile.

E   A hundred yards after passing a turn to the right, you see a sign on your left "Langford Farm and Cottage only - Private". There should also be a bridleway signpost here (GR.636957), so ignore the "Private" and turn left up a tarmac drive, passing some cottages on the right and a vast, new red brick house up to the left. Continue along a hedged green track to a gate with one of the CLA waymarks on it. Go through and follow a wide green track running along the valley and then curving round to the left below the rise on your left. When you get right round the base of this rise you will find a plethora of CLA waymarks - one charmingly indicating No Right of Way. Turn right here and walk up the other side of the valley, aiming at the telegraph pole on the skyline at the top. There is a faint, narrow track but it may not be visible in summer.

At the top go through the hunting gate ahead of you into a steeply sloping field. Cross it, following the line of telegraph poles until you are high enough to see across to a wide gap in the far hedge. Cross to this and go through the gate. Walk straight ahead, along a green track until this hits a stony one. Turn onto this and walk up to the top of the hill.

F   You emerge onto an open space where several tracks meet (GR.652965). This is Crete Hill. Turn left through a gate into a wide, hedged track and follow this for half a mile, going through one gate en route. Leave the track by a gate and keep straight along the top of the next field, hedge on your right.

G   When you reach a gate on your right, look into the corner of the little wood there and admire the new sculpture by Christine Angus. This was commissioned by a local farmer, Mr Will Best of Manor Farm, Godmanstone, and placed in position in 1987 with the help of Common Ground's New Milestones project (Note 27) (GR.655977).

Continue following the hedge on your right, through a gate and then, as the hedge curves slightly round to the right, watch out for a gate in the left hand corner of the hedge crossing down ahead. Cut the corner to walk across to this, go into the field and continue in the same direction as before. At the far end, leave the field by the hunting gate on the left, turn right and continue as before, now with the hedge once more on your right.

Now follow this line along the hedge for about a mile, passing through one gate and two gateways.

H   When you reach a new house and barn on your left, go through into the next field and turn left up the hedge to Farm Field Barn. You are now back on the Wessex Ridgeway and can follow the instructions in the main Guide back to Sydling St. Nicholas (E, F and G on page 24) and the Church.

oooOOOooo

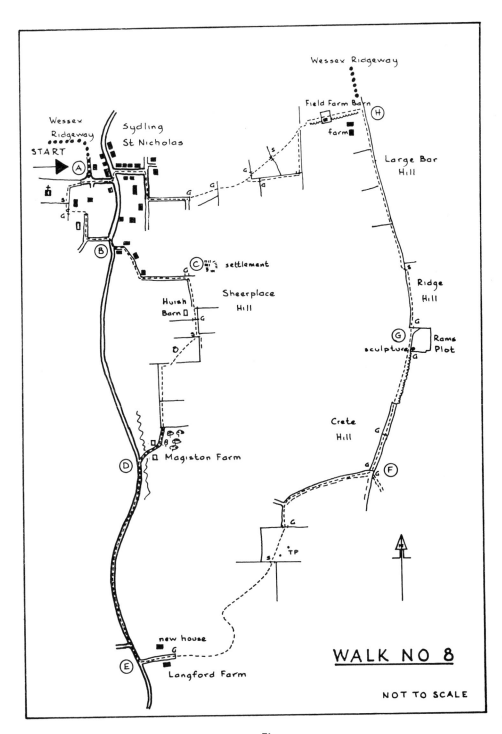

Wessex Ridgeway

Field Farm Barn

farm

Large Bar Hill

H

Wessex Ridgeway

START

Sydling St Nicholas

A

s

G

G

C settlement

G

Huish Barn

Sheerplace Hill

G

s

D

B

Ridge Hill

s

G

G

sculpture

Rams Plot

Crete Hill

G

G

F

G

s TP

Magiston Farm

D

new house

G

E

Langford Farm

WALK NO 8

NOT TO SCALE

71

Walk No. 9 - HOOKE PARK

A pleasant 6 mile circuit of valleys, streams and woods. There is one very muddy, but short, stretch. (Maps: Pathfinder 1298 (ST.40/50) & 1317 (SY.49/59); Landranger 194)

A   Start from Hooke village, reached by turning south-west off the A356 Maiden Newton to Crewkerne road, about 5 miles NW of Maiden Newton. Park by church (GR.535002). Leaving the church on your right, walk NW up the road for a quarter mile until a side road comes in from the right. This is where the Wessex Ridgeway joins your route for a short while.

Continue up the road, with a beautiful man-made lake on your right. After about 120 yards, where the road begins to climb and veer slightly left, there is a turn-round in front of a house down to the right where you might be able to get permission to leave any extra cars.

B   About 200 yards later you pass Hooke Court School on the left. Go through the first gate on the right hand side of the road (GR.530005) and follow the directions in the main guide, from D to E on page 30. This brings you to point C on this route.

C   On leaving the field, instead of following the Ridgeway to the right, cross the road with a right/ left and go through the gate on the far side. Follow the clear track across the field to a flat V corner and continue along the field edge with the hedge on your right and the wood, Coltwood Coppice, down to the left. Walking alone here, the writer has seen many deer and the occasional flights of wild duck.

Through the gate at the end of the field and straight on, with the hedge still on the right. The hedge coming in from the left marked the end of Coltwood Coppice, but behind and below it, the darker woods of Hooke Park can be seen curving away to the left. Splendid views to the west here.

Soon the track becomes stony and then leads through a gate into a third field with some interesting humps and bumps in it and a marshy looking spot in the middle. The track drops down towards a tree belt crossing it and here you pass a track going off to the left and negotiate what could be a very boggy spot in the trees.

From here the track becomes a double-hedged farm road running leftish uphill to Coltleigh Farm. Walk between the rather beautiful farmhouse on the left and a barn on the right. 100 yards later at the top of a rise, ignore a delicious looking track running downhill on the left and keep straight on until you reach a T junction with some trees on the right.

D   Turn left and follow the minor road downhill. From here you get a good view across the valley and can catch your first glimpse of Mapperton Manor (Note 28) down ahead. Mapperton Dairy is down to your left. Its entrance goes off from the next corner where your road bends right, past a row of splendid beech trees. After 200 yards the road bends left again and continues for a short distance to join the main road at a corner (GR.505999).

Walk straight ahead for about 500 yards, passing the drive entrance to the Manor on your left. (Notice the board telling you that the bridleway has been moved.)

E   Having passed on the right a pair of houses, two singles and then a second pair, look for a small gate on the left bearing a notice "New Right of Way". Enter the field and walk straight across, parallel to the Manor and its outbuildings over to the left. A gate at the end brings you out onto a tarmac drive where you turn right.

Walk along the drive for about 100 yards until it curves slightly left and then turns up to a rather gypsy-ish cottage on the right. Here you leave it and go through the metal gate ahead, marked "Game Reserve. Dogs on Lead". Walk straight ahead, following the valley as it curves round to the left, but keeping slightly up its left side - ignoring a rather tempting gate up to the right. A flat, green track soon leads you along and then, above a fascinating confluence of valleys, drops down to the right to a gate at the bottom.

F   The gate has a stile beside it (dropping you into some yuk!). Follow the earth and grass track south for about a quarter mile winding round the base of two hills up to the left. The wood is below to the right and you can hear the stream tinkling along its bottom.

Soon after you have gone through a gate, the track begins to drop down to the left and brings you to an open space where, again, two valleys join.

G   There are fords here, and a green track going off to the south along the east bank of a stream. But you stick to your track running hard round to the left and climbing uphill (GR.505987).

From here you simply follow the track for nearly a mile, up and downhill, through several gates, with trees up to the left and the stream down to the right. You can orientate yourself from the high (unnamed) hill above the stream to the right because you will be walking beside it and then round its eastern flank.

After passing a valley coming in from the left, where a stream runs underneath the track, you walk up and out into an open area, with no trees on the left. Along the same track, you pass a reedy little pond down to the right, then, at the bottom of a dip, another valley drops in from the left and this time the stream crosses your path and you have some (very wobbly) stepping stones to negotiate. After this, the wood on the right comes to an end and another starts on the left. This is the beginning of Hooke Park and now the steep slope is down to the left. Up to your right is an open slope with a wire fence running along its top.

H   Now the track leaves the valley and swings right, uphill with a hedge on the left (GR.517992). Go through a gate and follow the left hand hedge round to the left. Do not stick to the hedge but, as you rise, watch out for Burcombe farm ahead and steer towards it. Towards the end of the field you reach a steep drop and below it an earth track running left and right. Drop down to this, turn left and follow it down and round to the right. Go through a gate and onto a stony track with a stream occupying a little part of it. Pass a deserted cottage to your left and keep straight on along a lane for about 400 yards.

J   When your lane bears right (GR.520985), leave it and turn left into a wide track, with a little triangle on the right. Walk straight ahead to a stream. Cross this and go through a hunting gate. Follow the bed of the stream to a second hunting gate and then along a very muddy path uphill, leaving the stream below to the right. At the top of the slope a gate leads you (thankfully!) out into a field.

Walk over to the left hand edge and go through the first gate on your left. Then turn right and walk down to the bottom with the hedge to your right. Turn left for about 50 yards, watching out for a muddy little path down to a footbridge with a blue waymark on it.

K   This brings you into Hooke Park and all you have to do now is to keep walking north for half a mile.

At first the muddy track straight uphill is very obvious. At the far end of a clearing, you go straight over a track crossing and should follow the bridleway sign into a very overgrown stretch where the route is barely visible. However, parallel to this on the left is a neat little man-made path signposted "To Car Park" which you could probably follow without risking prosecution - as long as you do not lose sight of where you ought to be. If you do this, watch out for some steps on the right leading back to your route, topped by some wooden bars bearing a sign saying "Horses". From here, the path running north is much better.

The path ends at a sort of gazebo and here is another bridleway sign directing you straight ahead up a wide drive which sweeps round from the left.

Shortly after passing a Wildlife Reserve sign on the road, the drive forks. Take the right fork uphill to a gate out onto the road (GR.527999).

L   Here you do a left/right and walk along the road for half a mile back to Hooke.

oooOOOooo

WALK NO 9

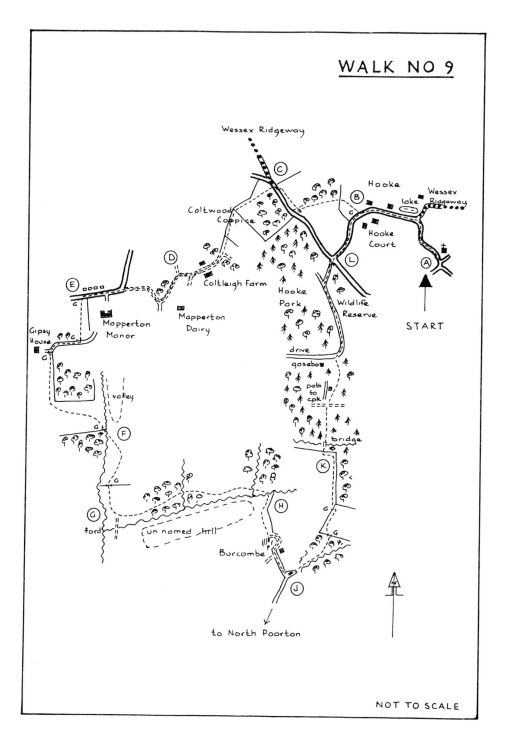

Wessex Ridgeway

Hooke

Wessex Ridgeway

Coltwood Coppice

Hooke Court

Coltleigh Farm

Wildlife Reserve

Mapperton Dairy

Hooke Park

Mapperton Manor

Gipsy House

START

valley

drive

gasebo

path to cpk

bridge

ford

un named hill

Burcombe

to North Poorton

NOT TO SCALE

Walk No. 10 - THE WARREN HILLS

Walked from Beaminster, this 6½ mile circuit affords glimpses of (and opportunities to visit) two stately homes as well as some beautiful, varied country and one spectacular view gained with very little effort.

N.B. Please do not take this walk with any dogs.

(Maps: Pathfinder 1298 (ST.40/50) and 1317 (SY.49/59); Landranger 193 and 194)

A   Start from the Market Square at Beaminster. Leave by the B3163 running east and walk along it for half a mile, passing and ignoring a tempting green lane running down to the right. Shortly after, turn right down a lane with a small green triangle at its mouth. There should be a bridleway post here (GR.488007).

B   At the end of the lane go through the left hand (metal) of two gates - signposted 'Bridleway' and turn left. Follow the discernible little path just below the 'shelf' up to the left. You have nearly three quarters of a mile along the valley, always keeping the stream down below to the right, and walking gate to gate. After encountering a metal gate with a splendid new stile a few feet beyond it, and then, keeping to the same line and passing below a little rough enclosure up to the left, you go through a gateway in the hedge and begin watching out for a wide V-shaped opening in the fence below to the right (GR.502001).

C   Walk down to this, over a stile, a footbridge and a second stile up to the left. Then walk diagonally left up the field, aiming at the telegraph pole up in the hedge on the skyline.

In the top corner of the field, cross the stile on your right, walk along the hedge on your left for about 30 feet and go through the gate on the left. Walk down the headland of the next field, hedge on left, and out onto the road.

D   Looking across half left from here you can see Mapperton Manor (Note 28). To visit it, turn left and walk along the road to the entrance.

Otherwise turn right and walk along the road for a quarter mile, ignoring a highly tempting green track going down to the right.

E   The entrance to the lane into which you turn right is guarded by a solitary sycamore, known as the Posy Tree, and the lane you are about to enter is Dead Mans Lane (note 28 again). Follow the lane, rising slowly and keep left at the top, passing on your right a notice on a gate enjoining walkers to keep to the footpath (GR.493997).

F   After the lane has veered left, you come to a sharp right turn and here there may be problems. If you find the lane clear, follow it, first right, then left until it emerges into the open. Then continue, hedge on right, to the gate in the corner (G).

BUT, if you find the lane full of undergrowth at F, do NOT attempt it as it becomes much worse further on. Instead, go through the gate in front of you, turn right and follow the outside of the lane hedge to the gate into a second field and then on until you spot where the lane emerges. Then turn down to the gate in the corner.

It must be stressed that there is no right of way in the first field but the farmer will not object to walkers as long as they are without dogs and keep to the top edge.

G   From this gate there is a spectacular view across Marshwood Vale and into East Devon. Quarter right on the skyline you can see the dark Lewesdon Hill and behind it the flat top and steep drop of Pilsdon Pen (Note 20). You are on South Warren Hill and North Warren Hill is to the right. The gate you are leaning on, wooden-framed with slender, vertical iron bars is known as a Dorset gate and these are becoming rather rare. It carries a nice Please/Thank You request to walkers.

Once through the gate, turn left. The green shelf you are on runs up to the skyline. Below it is a track following the contour and rising to a gate on the skyline. Below that again is a narrow sheep track leading towards some trees at a lower point on the hill and this is the one you should follow.

However, you can make a little detour here to gaze upon the site of another Plague landmark - the site of the mass grave for victims - in a small tree plantation. There is no evidence on the ground there, but it is worth walking along the ridge as far as you feel inclined, just to see where it is, particularly as the bridleway followed by the walk will take you below the ridge.

So, for the detour, turn left at the Dorset gate and walk along the top to the fence on the horizon. Follow the fence along to the gate and continue alongside the fence into the next field. At the end, go through the left hand one of a pair of gates and continue as far as you like. Then walk back to the first gate and drop down to the sheep track.

At the next gate take the lower of two little paths forking ahead. This becomes a wide, green shelf swinging right, left and right again, hugging the hill.

When another shelf comes in from behind you on the left, you can either drop down into a hollow lane ahead for about 100 yards, or continue along the green shelf above it.

When you come out into a clearing there is a splendid view half left across to the coastal ridge, with Thorncombe Beacon and Golden Cap on the skyline. Down ahead is another deep, hollow lane. This is the true line of the bridleway but it is fenced off at the moment and common custom for years has been to go through the gate quarter right ahead, walk down the left hand headland of the field, left at the bottom and out onto the road. Turn right.

H   This is the main B3066 Beaminster/Bridport road and is lethal, with the turns going the wrong way for walkers. Follow it for 200 yards, take the left turn on the bend signposted Netherbury, and turn left again into the hedged lane at the bottom of the slope (GR.479991).

J   After about 200 yards, the hedge on your right (and the mud) comes to an end at a gate. Go through and keep straight on, along the headland of two fields, with the hedge first on your left, then on your right. At the end of the second field, go through the gate, turn right and follow the earth track, hedge on right. The big house you can see across the valley is Slape Manor.

Your hedge goes off to the right but you keep straight on, passing between a clump of trees on the right and two singles up to the left, and following the track slightly round to the right and down to a gate. Through this and walk quarter right down into the far corner.

Turn right through a gate and walk for quarter of a mile along a hedged and fenced lane with the River Brit down on your left. If it is Spring, watch for a blossom-filled orchard on the left. This area was once farmed for its orchards. The lane is called Hatchlands Lane and on the way you pass the sumptuous property of Hatchlands on the right. The lane ends at a crossroads in Netherbury. Go straight across and walk up the road until it swings round to the right (GR.473993).

K   Turn left and follow the footpath fingerpost down a dank little path to the weir. Turn right over it, left along the river bank (in a nice little corner where the writer, for one, would enjoy a tea stop) and up to a kissing gate in the corner. Then straight uphill to a T-junction. Turn right here and walk straight on, along the edge of the churchyard, passing the church of St Mary on your left. This was restored in the nineteenth century but is otherwise mainly medieval and contains a memorial to the family of Sir Thomas More, whose effigy bears an S.S. collar worn by nobles loyal to the Lancastrian cause in the 14th century.

The path widens, with a wire fence on the left, and ends at a kissing gate leading out into a field. Follow the discernible little path curving slightly left along the bottom, with a fence and some splendid trees on your right. Go over the stile at the end and continue along a hedged track. After a short distance a lane comes in from the left and then you drop down to a gate and out into an open space.

Over to the left is a rather attractive ruined house with a barn called Clenham. Keep along the right hand edge of the open space and turn right through a gate with a stile beside it and follow the drive round to the left. Walk along it for a couple of hundred yards until it veers left uphill. Then leave it and walk straight ahead into a grass and earth track above the Brit with a hedge on the left and a wood on the right.

L   After about 400 yards watch out for a spaced-out group of trees up to the left and then a stile in the hedge. This will take you up to the Rhodes-Moorhouse cemetery (Note 30) and it is worth walking up to see it and then returning to your route at approximately GR.474004.

As you continue along the valley, a path comes in from the wood on your right. This would take you down into the grounds of Parnham House - well worth a visit (Note 29). As you emerge through a gate into an open space, keep close to the hedge on your left but turn to look across to Parnham back down to the right. After passing some rough ground, the hedge on the left leaves you and you walk straight across a field along a discernible path to the gate at the far end.

Keep to the bottom edge of the next field with the trees on the right and drop down to a stony road winding in from the right. Go through a gate below a house up to the left and into a double-hedged lane and follow this back into Beaminster. Turn right at The Eight Bells pub and walk up into the Market Square.

oooOOOooo

Note: This walk was devised by Misses Joy Atkinson and Teddy Edwards of Beaminster who have patiently walked it with the writer and friends and again with her and her tape-recorder for the final recce.

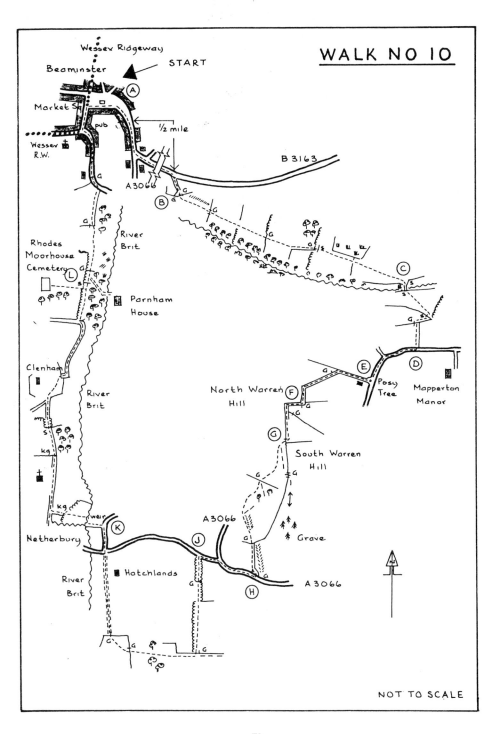

WALK NO 10

Wesser Ridgeway
Beaminster
START
Market St
pub
½ mile
Wesser
R.W.
A3066
B 3163
B
River
Brit
Rhodes
Moorhouse
Cemetery
L
Parnham
House
Clenham
River
Brit
kg
kg
weir
Netherbury
K
River
Brit
Hatchlands
A3066
J
C
Mapperton
Manor
Posy
Tree
E
D
North Warren
Hill
F
G
South Warren
Hill
Grave
A3066
H

NOT TO SCALE

Walk No. 11 - HORN HILL AND LEWESDON from Broadwindsor

This 6 mile circle involves one long, slow climb and two short, steep ones. Its two high points provide splendid views in several directions and on the way you will be enjoying a flower-bedecked lane, a pleasant valley and two splendid hills. (Maps: Pathfinder 1298 (ST.40/50); Landranger Sheet 183)

Start from Broadwindsor. If arriving by one car, find a suitable spot to park. If more cars are involved, it might be advisable to obtain permission to park at the village hall (the Comrades Hall) at GR.438026. The caretaker is Mrs Audrey Woodley of 10 Fullers (Tel. Broadwindsor 68753). It would also be nice to offer a small contribution to village hall funds.

A   From the hall, take the road running north signposted 'Mosterton' and take the first turn right at the end of a wall. This is Common Water Lane and you will be on it for one and a half miles. After one or two houses, it changes from a road to a lane. It starts by rising slightly and, just before it starts to dip, you can get your first view across to the right, at a large gateway. Quarter right is Lewesdon Hill, with the trees on it, and quarter left is Waddon Hill. The Wessex Ridgeway runs along this side of both and you will be returning to Broadwindsor along it. All the way along this lane you will catch views through gates on either side.

At the bottom of the dip, just past Cottage Farm on the right, you keep right at a lane fork and, a few yards later, have a peep over the gate on the left at a pleasant little lake harbouring swans and wild duck.

After another slight rise and fall you begin the last climb up to Horn Hill and the lane begins to close in on you with higher banks.

B   Halfway up a slight curve to the left and nearly opposite to a metal gate which looks like the end of a bedstead, you will see a DCC bridleway post near a tree on the right, with a little path climbing the bank beside it (GR.461029). Turn onto this and follow the path down and round to the left.

If you can contrive to do this walk in May you will find the wood (Foxholes Plantation on the map) a total glory of bluebells.

C   Ignore the hunting gate down to the right and continue along the path for about 200 yards until it turns sharply left uphill to another hunting gate. Here you turn right down to a stile and over. Walk down the field with the hedge on your left, passing one gate and turning left through a second one near the bottom.

Walk ahead down towards the valley, aiming at the farm buildings on the rise beyond the trees. At the bottom of the slope, walk between a long, gorse covered bank concealing a streamlet and a line of scrubby little trees running down to the right. Keep your line along the top edge of the scrub to the right and you will soon find yourself walking along a wide, green track. This leads into another track which goes down to a gated bridge on the right (GR.463021).

D   Cross the bridge and walk up the loose-stone drive to Horn Park Farm, emerging past a house on the left, into the yard, with a tarted up little house called Pigeon Cottage quarter right ahead. Keep straight ahead here, up a slope, past a second farmyard and a barn and out into a field.

Cross the field diagonally left and keep the same line down the next field. Here you go through into the third field to find the exit gate down in the corner to the left.

80

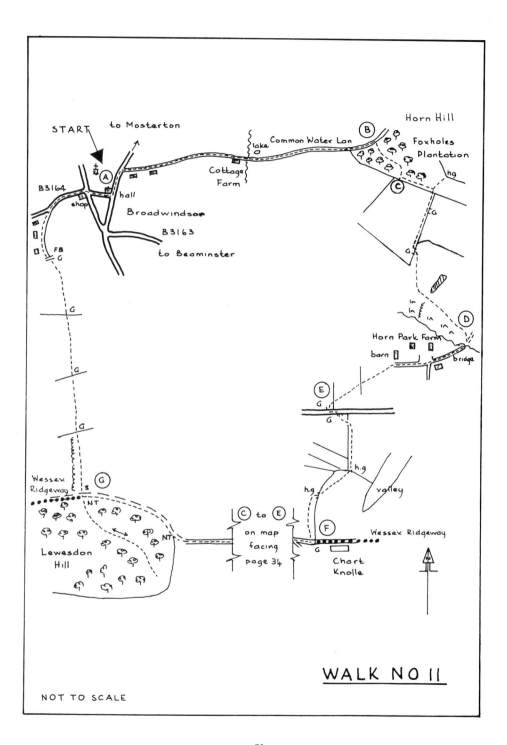

START

to Mosterton

Horn Hill

Common Water Lan

lake

(B)

Foxholes Plantation

hg

B3164

(A)

hall

shop

Cottage Farm

(C)

G

Broadwindsor

B3163

to Beaminster

G

FB
G

G

G

G

(D)

Horn Park Farm

barn

bridge

(E)
G

G

Wessex Ridgeway

(G)
s

NT

NT

h.g

valley

h.g

Lewesdon Hill

(C) to (E)

on map facing page 34

(F)
G

Wessex Ridgeway

Chart Knolle

N

WALK NO 11

NOT TO SCALE

E   Cross the road and enter the field on the other side by the gate a few yards to the left. Walk left across the corner into the adjoining field, turn right and walk uphill, with the hedge on your right.

As you climb, the house at Chart Knolle comes into view, at the head of the little valley running along below you. At this point you will be walking along a narrow path between what will be some formidable scrub and undergrowth in the summer. Your life will be saved when you spot the hunting gate up in the corner ahead. Go through this and follow the contour straight ahead to a metal hunting gate. Through this, turn left and walk up to the corner nearest to the house - Chart Knolle at F (GR.456015).

F   Do not go through the gate on the left, as you are now on the Wessex Ridgeway and will be turning right. Before doing so, turn round and look back across the valley you have just crossed, where you will be able to see Horn Hill up the other side.

Now follow the directions for the Wessex Ridgeway, C and D, on page 34 (F to G on this map).

At G take the footpath up to the left to the top of Lewesdon Hill. This brings you out on the SE corner of the ridge where you will enjoy a spectacular view to the east and to the south across Marshwood Vale to the hills above the coast.

Return to G the same way and then go over the stile facing you across the Wessex Ridgeway route.

Walk down the first field with a "hedge" of tall beech trees on your left. At the end, go through a gap in the wire and ford the yuk on the wobbly stones lying in it to the gate. Keep the same line down the next two fields, gate to gate.

The fourth field drops down on both sides but you keep to the high ground in the centre, straight ahead until you spot the gate below you. Here you cross a small bridge and then, keeping right, walk past some houses on the left. Turn right and walk up the hill into Broadwindsor. On your way, pause at the Old Chapel on your right and pop into the Dorset Pine Craft workshop to meet a local craftsman.

From the village shop, turn half right, following the one-way street arrows, and walk back to the Comrades Hall.

oooOOOooo

NOTES OF PLACES OF INTEREST

I ON THE RIDGEWAY

SECTION I

1   **Ashmore**
Highest village in Dorset. Beautiful (never drying-up) village pond complete with Muscovy ducks and cedar tree, plus old barn and attractive old buildings. It holds a Midsummer merrymaking called "Filly Loo" which has, since the 1920's, included morris dancing by local "sides" such as the Dorset Trumph and the White Horse Morris Dancers and music by such entrepreneurs as the Hambledon Hop Step Band and a fiddler who has played annually at the Filly Loo for over 30 years. The celebrations end with a Circassion circle round the torchlit pond.

There have been no pubs in the village since the early 19th century when they were closed by one Luke Howard, a Quaker who came to Ashmore from London around 1800.

There is also a connection with Lord Rutherford, of atom-splitting fame. His daughter used to spend holidays in the village and they were often seen there together. She died in the Thirties and - then Mrs Howard Fowler - is buried in Ashmore Churchyard.

2   **Shroton**
The name comes from Old English, meaning "sheriff's estate". At the time of the Domesday Book, Shroton belonged to Baldwin of Exeter, Sheriff of Devon. In the thirteenth century it was owned by the Courtenays, Earls of Devon, hence its present alternative name of IWERNE COURTNEY, i.e. "estate on the River Iwerne belonging to the Courtenay family".

Shroton church was the scene of the incarceration by Cromwell's forces of 300 "Dorset Clubmen", a band of locals formed to oppose both sides in the Civil War to prevent plunder by either. They were released after promising "to be very dutiful for time to come".

3   **Hambledon Hill**
There are two ancient monuments on the Hill. The first is a neolithic causewayed camp of which little remains except three crossdykes. Neolithic pottery, axes, arrowheads, cattle bones and two human skulls have been found there.

The second is a magnificent Iron Age hill fort commanding a superb view over Blackmoor Vale. A neolithic long barrow crosses its central ridge. The route does not actually take walkers through the fort but the way into it will be indicated in the Guide and on the map.

4   **Hod Hill**
The Iron Age hill fort on Hod is the largest in the county - contrary to appearance, larger even than Maiden Castle. Celtic votive model shields have been found there and it is believed to have been one of those invested by Vespasian, possibly by ballista fire with no direct assault. The Romans then, somewhat unusually, established a fort in the north-west corner and, according to evidence, occupied it from 43 to 51 AD.

5   **Shillingstone**
Its other name, Shilling Okeford, comes from the twelfth century lords of the manor, the Eskellings, and Okeford from the fords in the old oak forest of Blackmoor Vale. At one time it boasted the tallest - 110 feet - most popular maypole in Dorset, celebrated in verse by the Dorset poet, William Barnes. Three times restored, it was finally taken down in 1938. In the centre of the village stands an old market cross which was renewed as a Jubilee memorial for Queen Victoria's Jubilee.

6   Ringmoor

A small Romano-British settlement owned by the National Trust and beautifully sited on the side of Ibberton Long Down. Entry is past a lovely old dewpond and still visible are the embanked trackways into the settlement and the bank and ditch surrounding possible hut platforms.

7   Rawlesbury Camp

An Iron Age fort on Bulbarrow Hill, believed to have been first occupied from the mid third century BC. Bulbarrow is the second highest hill in Dorset - 902 feet. It is believed to have been the site of one of the Armada Beacons in 1588 as well as part of the hilltop telegraph system in the Napoleonic Wars.

8   The Dorsetshire Gap

A hollow pass in the chalk scarp of Nordon Hill and a meeting place of many trackways. It is uncertain whether the Gap was originally man-made or whether it started life as a natural dip in the scarp, deepened by wind and water and subsequently adopted by man as a road crossing. Either way it would then have been further deepened by traffic from various directions. The Gap is known to have been an important road crossing in the Middle Ages and the earliest Ordnance Survey maps indicate that it was still an important link in the nineteenth century road system. However, the fact that there are so many prehistoric remains in the immediate vicinity suggest that its history goes much further back - into pre-Roman times.

Be that as it may, the Gap today is a very special place, with its own particular form of magic. N.B. Please sign the book you will find in the green tin.

9   Folly

Once the Folly Inn, a resting place for the drovers using the network of old drove roads on and around this section of the route. Was not closed until sometime in the fifties or sixties and is now a private house.

10   Giants Head

So called because it is on the top of the hill on whose slope the famous Cerne Giant is carved. 180 feet tall, the Giant is generally thought to represent Hercules but there are legends suggesting an older god. He cannot be seen from the top of the hill, nor in his full glory from Cerne Abbas at the bottom and needs to be viewed from the heights on the far side of the Cerne Valley.

At the Giants Head there is a pleasant caravan site where B & B can be obtained and where there is a shop open in the summer. The old 1:25000 map still shows it as an inn; but it has not been one since 1911 when it was closed for being an unruly house. You can pitch your tent here, eat a snack at the bar in the evening, and the landlord will give you breakfast or you can rent a caravan for the night. A camping barn is planned.

11   Cerne Abbas

A pretty little town, named from the River Cerne (from Celtic "carn" meaning "cairn"), very much of a "honeypot" in the summer and at holiday times. Has medieval houses, a 14th century tithe barn, an early Christian wishing-well, the Abbey ruins and The Giant. The Abbey was founded in the 9th century and re-founded as a Benedictine one in about 987. There is a network of little back lanes which wander around, over and along the River Cerne and the Town Pond is usually embellished with Muscovy ducks.

SECTION III

12 Up Cerne
Boasts a 16th century gabled manor house built by Sir Robert Mellor as an extension of an existing medieval hall. It is not open to the public but can be viewed from the road. The church, adjoining the house, has a medieval chancel, but was otherwise greatly restored in the 19th century.

13 Sydling St Nicholas
The name means "place at the large ridge" from Old English "sid" meaning "large" and "hlinc" = a ridge. A very attractive village not massively infected with tourists in summer. The Sydling Water flows through it in three separate streams so that many of the cottages are reached by little bridges. The Saxons settled it in the 7th and 8th centuries an in 933 AD the land was given to the Benedictine monks at Milton Abbey. The chestnut tree, where the route crosses to walk up to the church, was planted in 1911. The 15th century church, St Nicholas, has a fireplace in the porch, a wagon roof in the nave, some box pews and a squint with an odd stone corbel. The yew trees are reputed to be over 1,000 years old.

14 Maiden Newton
A Domesday Book village at the junction of the Rivers Hooke and Frome. St Mary's Church has an original Norman door, believed to be the oldest door in England. The site of a Roman villa, complete with tessellated pavements and found east of the village early in the 19th century, has been lost sight of! Sylvia Townsend Warner lived here and the Queen spent a night in the royal train there in 1952 on a visit to the west.

SECTION IV

15 Hooke Park
A working Woodland Centre in Hooke Park is a new venture by the Parnham Trust. It will be Britain's first school to specialise in woodland industry. There is one bridle path right through the Park and some other paths are being constructed through the woodland, for use by ticket holders on Wednesdays and Sundays from April to October. Once the School is built, visitors will be able to watch woodwork from a gallery in the workshops.

16 Toller Whelme
Situated at the river spring of the Toller Stream (now called the Hooke), this is no longer even a hamlet - just a beautiful 16th century manor house with a 15th century porch, once a part of the Forde Abbey demesne. Its name is of interest as it means "source of the River Toller", the word "whelme" deriving from "aewielm", Old English for "river spring". Described most poetically by Frederick Treves in 1906 (Highways and Byways in Dorset) as "sleeping its last sleep. There is no village, no hamlet - not even the sight of living men". This last is no longer true as the manor house is now flourishing under private ownership - but not open to the public.

17 Beaminster
Thomas Hardy's "Emminster", flushed by the river Brit. Much of the town was burned down, twice in the 17th century and once in the 18th century, so the market place consists mostly of 17th and 18th century houses. The town was the centre of the district which produced Blue Vinney cheese. St Mary's Church, passed on the route out of town, is of Ham Hill stone and is early 16th century with pinnacles and sculpture over its west door. Nearby are some 17th century almshouses.

SECTION V

18 Stoke Knapp

A place of no particular interest except for the fact that Timperley & Brill believed that the Great Ridgeway may have had two alternative routes: a summer one which followed the ridge to the north of Beaminster and then kept straight on into Broadwindsor; and another which left the ridge by what is now a bridle way running south up to Stoke Knapp and thence past Lewesdon and along the present motor road up Cockpit Hill to the foot of Pilsdon Pen. (see "Ancient Trackways of Wessex")

The word "knap" means either the unopened head of a potato or a small hillock rising - presumably the latter in this case as it lies at the foot of both Waddon and Lewesdon Hills.

19 Broadwindsor

Has two main claims to fame: firstly that Thomas Fuller was vicar from 1634 until 1650 and then, after a Cromwellian interlude, again from 1660 to 1661, and for secondly that it provided an overnight hiding place at the Castle Inn for the night of 23rd-24th September 1651 for Charles II after the Battle of Worcester. The Inn was burned down in 1856.

The church, St John the Baptist, is partly Norman, including the font, with a 15th century tower which contains three very ancient bells.

20 Pilsdon Pen

At 909 feet, the highest hill in Dorset, crowned with an 8 acre Iron Age hill fort. Its name derives from two sources: Old English "pil" meaning "stake" and "dun" meaning "hill", and Celtic "penn" meaning "hill".

Excavation has uncovered Iron Age hut sites, including one which might have been used as a goldsmith's workshop, as a crucible was found with beads of gold stuck to it. A rectangular building, erected in the centre during the first century BC had been reduced to four low banks by the end of the Iron Age. The hill fort is believed to have been still occupied when the Romans arrived in Britain and it was captured by Vespasian in AD43. It is now owned by the National Trust.

SECTION VI

21 Lamberts Castle

Iron Age hill fort with round barrow now owned by the National Trust. Believed to have been named after King Lambert, i.e. King Canute. The summit is a vast plateau, large enough to absorb holiday visitors without any overcrowding and with extensive views into Dartmoor to the west and over to Chesil Bank to the east. One of the 13 Armada Beacon sites listed by the historian Hutchins was at Hawkchurch in Devon, but is believed to have been Lambert's Castle.

22 Coneys Castle

An Iron Age fort of a completely different character, also owned by the National Trust. It used to be known to the locals as "Happy Fields" and this is the clue to its atmosphere. Not very large, with a tree-filled hollow in the centre, it has an almost 'cosy' feel and in spring is a mass of bluebells. There is no view to the west and that to the east, across Marshwood Vale, is only discernible through the trees along its edge. It is believed to have been used as a camp by Egbert when fighting the Danes in AD 833.

23 Lyme Regis

A very attractive and still unspoiled little town, once a commercial port. The route down into it passes a variety of old mills, once driven by the river Lim and the latter wanders down between the houses alongside the walkers as they march towards the coast.

Lyme Regis is one of the oldest boroughs in England, having been enfranchised by Edward I in 1279. In the Civil War it stood up against a Royalist force for two months but in 1685 it took the wrong side when it welcomed Monmouth who landed there in that year- reputedly accompanied by Daniel Defoe. After Monnouth's defeat Nemesis fell on Lyme and welve local men were hanged on the beach.

Jane Austen was a frequent visitor and the Cobb, an ancient 600 foot quay, was the scene of Louisa Musgrove's fall. Another claim to fame was the discovery by the twelve year old Mary Anning of the icthysaurus at Black Ven in 1811. It took her around ten years to uncover it completely and the British Museum paid her £23 for her work.

II ON THE CIRCULAR WALKS

24 Milton Abbas

The village now often cited as the first example of "town Planning". In the late 18th century the first Earl of Dorchester razed the original market town, built a model village out of sight of his own residence and forcibly rehoused the villagers there. History does not relate what happened to them while the building was going on.

The Abbey was founded in 932 by King Athelstan as a college for canons, and refounded as a Benedictine monastery by King Edgar in 938. The Abbey Church is 14th and 15th century and has no nave because the Dissolution occurred before it was started. The main house was built in 1771 for the Earl and is now Milton Abbey School.

In the woods above the Abbey is St Catherine's Chapel, a Saxon chapel rebuilt by the Normans. It became a labourer's cottage during the 19th century, then a carpenter's workshop and then a lumber store. Restored this century, it is now owned by Salisbury Diocese and regular services are held there.

25 Ansty

Ansty is a straggly village made up of several settlements - Higher Ansty, Lower Ansty, Little Ansty or Pleck and Ansty Cross. It is remarkable mainly for the occasional ceremonial award on 'Randy Day' to the most suitable Village Virgin, and for the Fox Inn, a very popular eating-place. The most attractive section is probably Aller which boasts some splendid gardens and a series of recently man-made lakes teeming with bird life. The name Ansty derives from Old English "anstiga" meaning "narrow footpath".

Worth visiting is the garden at Ivy Cottage - open every Thursday and some Sundays from 1st April to 30th September. Suggest first telephoning Milton Abbas 880053 for information and directions (from Fox Inn).

26 Binghams Melcombe

The tiny hamlet of Binghams Melcombe was held from the King by one Robert de Oilly at the time of the Domesday Book. The little church of St Andrew is 14th of 15th century and the Manor House (unfortunately not open to the public), which can only be glimpsed from the footpath, is 15th century and is one of the best examples in the county of a medieval manor. It was owned by the Bingham family - one of whose ancestors fought at Lepanto in 1571 - for six centuries until the end of the 19th. The gardens are remarkable for a massive yew hedge, 18 feet thick, which can be viewed from the path. The most romantic description of the almost invisible house can be gleaned from Frederick Treves' "Highways and Byways in Dorset", Chapter VII.

27 New Milestones Project

This is one of the projects being promoted by COMMON GROUND, a body set up in 1983 to promote - in their words- "the importance of our common cultural heritage - common plants and animals, familiar and local places, local distinctiveness and our links with the past". They work through local people and try to encourage practical links with those involved in the arts. They have been able to help one or two local communities to prepare their own Parish Maps.

The New Milestones Project is designed to encourage local communities to express their affection for particular spots by means of carfully placed sculptures in the countryside. These are commissioned locally, paid for by local subscription and donation and their themes and locations chosen after local consultation.

The sculpture on Walk No. 8, by Christine Angus, was finished in May 1988. It is on land owned by Mr Will Best, a well-known organic farmer, of Manor Farm, Godmanstone.

28 Mapperton Manor

A Tudor house, altered and enlarged in the 17th century, with Elizabethan plaster ceilings, in 17th and 18th century panelling and vast Jacobean overmantels. Eagle-crested piers guard the entrance to the main courtyard and the gardens are terraced down to the stream. The house was built by one Robert Morgan who, according to Frederick Treves, was exempted by Henry VIII from doffing his hat in the royal presence because of "diverse infirmities which he has in his hedde". The house is open to th public in the afternoons from April to October inclusive.

The village of Mapperton was deserted during the Great Plague and is now only a hamlet. In a nearby lane can now be seen the Posy Tree, the sycamore which has succeeded the oak at whose feet were laid posies to ward off the plague. The bodies of the plague victims were carried down the lane, to be left on the parish boundary and later taken down Dead Man's Lane (now a bridleway) for burial on South Warren Hill.

29 Parnham House

Originally built on a medieval plan by the Strode family in the 15th century, the house was rebuilt by them in the 16th century and again, still by the same family, in the 17th century when a large kitchen block was added. They were at it again in the 18th century, before the house was acquired in 1764 by the Oglander family in the Isle of Wight. The latter in their turn, added the south front designed by John Nash in 1810. The strode family were originally yeoman who flourished by means of good farming, astute purchases and strategic marriages. Coker, in his survey of Dorsetshire, notes that the Strodes flourished there in "Knights Degree, even from before the Date of antient Evidence until this present, and much bettered their Estates".

From 1955 to 1976 Parnham House belonged to the National Association for Mental Health but in 1976 it was acquired by John Makepeace and now houses his famous School for Craftsmen in Wood. John Makepeace has a worldwide reputation as a furniture maker, producing mostly commissioned pieces. The school houses ten pupils and offers two scholarships. It is now run as a non-profit making educational charity, the Parnham Trust. The workshops, house, gardens and restaurant are open to the public on Wednesdays and Sundays from Easter to October.

30 Rhodes-Moorhouse Cemetery

Above Parnham House (once the home of the Rhodes-Moorhouse family) and reached by a public right of way, this little private cemetery is well worth a visit. It contains the grave of the first airman ever to be awarded the Victoria Cross, Lieutenant William Barnard Rhodes-Moorhouse, killed in France in 1915, and those of his parents and of his brother. His wife, Linda Rhodes-Moorhouse, was also a pilot and her ashes were taken to the hill, likewise those of his two sisters. His son, Flight Lieutenant William Rhodes-Moorhouse DFC, was shot down in the Battle of Britain in September 1940 and his ashes are buried in the cemetery beside his father.

A quiet and lonely place - not to be missed.

BOOKS TO READ

The Wessex Ridgeway, Alan Proctor, The Ramblers Association (£3 inc p+p) from 1-5 Wandsworth Road, London SW8 2XX.

Ordnance Survey Landranger Guide to Dorset, published 1987 (contains four circular walks from Wessex Ridgeway - see below)

Ashley, Harry, *The Dorset Village Book*, Countryside Books 1984.

Ashley, Harry, *Dorset Inns*, Countryside Books 1987.

Brown, Mary, *Dorset: Customs, Curiosities and Country Lore*, Ensign Publications 1990.

Coker, John, *Survey of Dorsetshire*, Facsimile of 1732 edition. Dorset Publishing Co. 1980.

Creed, Sylvia, *Dorset's Western Vale*, Dorset Publishing Co. 1987.

David, Joy (editor), *The Hidden Places of Somerset: Avon and Dorset*, Maps Marketing Ltd 1989.

Draper, Jo, *Dorset. The Complete Guide*, Dovecote Press 1987.

Gant, Roland, *Dorset Villages*, Robert Hale 1980.

Good, Ronald, *The Old Roads of Dorset*, Horace G. Commin Ltd 1966.

Good, Ronald, *The Lost Villages of Dorset*, Dovecote Press 1979.

Hawkins, Desmond, *Cranborne Chase*, Gollancz 1980.

Jesty, Chris, *A Guide to the West Dorset Countryside*, Dovecote Press 1986.

Legg, Rodney, *Dorset National Trust Guide,* Dorset Publishing Co. 1992.

Legg, Rodney, *Literary Dorset*, Dorset Publishing Co. 1990.

Legg, Rodney, *Mysterious Dorset*, Dorset Publishing Co. 1987.

Legg, Rodney, *National Trust Dorset,* Dorset Publishing Co. 1987.

Mee, Arthur, *Dorset*, Hodder & Stoughton 1967.

Moule, H.J., *Old Dorset*, Cassell 1893.

Osborn, George, *Dorset Curiosities*, Dovecote Press 1986/87.

Pitfield, F.P., *Hardy's Wessex Locations,* Dorset Publishing Co. 1992.

Pitt-Rivers, Michael, *Shell Guide: Dorset*, Faber 1966.

Poole, Alison & Williams, Michael, *Unknown Dorset*, Bossinney Books 1989.

Taylor, Christopher, *The Making of the English Landscape - Dorset*, Hodder & Stoughton 1970.

Timperley, H.W & Brill, Edith, *Ancient Trackways of Wessex*, Phoenix House 1965.

Treves, Frederick, *Highways and Byways in Dorset*, Macmillan 1935.

Wansborough, Richeldis, *The Tale of Milton Abbas*, Dorset Publishing Co. 1974.

Wright, Geoffrey N., *Roads and Trackways of Wessex*, Moorland Publishing Co. 1988.

Recommended Walks from OS Landranger Guide:

SECTION I of Ridgeway - OS Walk No.7
A 5 mile walk from Plush.
Includes 2 miles along Ridgeway.

SECTION II of Ridgeway - OS Walk No.8
An 8 mile figure of eight from Bulbarrow Hill.
(Covers some of same ground as Ridgeway Walks Nos. 4 & 5)

SECTION III of Ridgeway - OS Walk No. 6
7 miles from Watts Hill.
Includes 1½ miles along Ridgeway.

SECTION IV of Ridgeway - OS Walk No. 1
6 miles from Coneys Castle.
Includes 3 miles along Ridgeway.

It will be noted that there are no circular walks in the far west. But there are some excellent leaflets by the Charmouth Heritage Coast Centre describing walks around Wootton Fitzpaine and Lyme Regis. These can be obtained from:

> The County Planning Office
> Dorset County Council
> County Hall
> Dorchester DT1 1XJ

They will also supply other information on Guided Walks etc. Please enclose a s.a.e.

ACCOMMODATION
Suggestions - East to West

Many places on this list do not provide evening meals, but will advise on local eating places. Walkers are advised to enquire and book in advance.

Tollard Royal
King John Hotel, Tollard Royal, Salisbury, Wiltshire (0725 207)
Not in Dorset but walkers might start here.

Shillingstone
The Willows, 5 Blandford Road, Shillingstone, Blandford DT11 0SG (0258 861167)
Bere Marsh House, Shillingstone, Blandford DT11 9BT (0258 861133)
Seymer Arms, Cookswell, Shillingstone, Blandford DT11 0QZ (0258 860488)

Ibberton
Mrs D.W. Old, Manor House Farm, Ibberton, Blandford DT11 0EN (0258 817349)

Ansty
The Fox Inn, Ansty, Dorchester DT2 7PN (0258 880328)
'Badgers Sett', Cross Lanes, Melcombe Bingham, Dorchester DT2 7PF (0258 880697)

For campers: Giants Head Farm, Old Sherborne Road, Cerne Abbas, Dorchester DT2 7TR (0300 341242)
Open April-October inclusive.

Cerne Abbas
The New Inn, 14 Long Street, Cerne Abbas, Dorchester DT2 7JF (0300 341274)
The Old Market House, 25 Long Street, Cerne Abbas, Dorchester DT2 7JG (0300 341680)
Mrs M.J. English, 47 Long Street, Cerne Abbas, Dorchester DT2 7JG (0300 341377)
Mr & Mrs Simmonds, Sound O' Water, 16 Duck Street, Cerne Abbas, Dorchester (0300 341435)
 (Double rooms only. William Barnes fans!)
Mrs R.J. Munn, The Singing Kettle, 7 Long Street, Cerne Abbas, Dorchester (0300 341349)

Sydling St Nicholas
Mrs Ann Barker, 1 The Green, Sydling St Nicholas (0300 341665)
Mrs T. Barraclough, Magiston Farm, Sydling St Nicholas (0300 20295)
 (1 mile south of village; reachable by public footpath)

Maiden Newton
Mr & Mrs J. Coates, Castle Inn, Dorchester Road, Maiden Newton DT2 0BG (0300 20481)

Lower Kingcombe
The Kingcombe Centre, Lower Kingcombe, Toller Porcorum, Dorchester DT2 0EQ. (0300 20684)

Beaminster
The Eight Bells Inn, Church Street, Beaminster DT8 3AZ (0308 863241)
The Knapp Inn, 23 Clay Lane, Beaminster DT8 3BU (0308 862408)
Jenny Wren's, 1 Hogshill Street, Beaminster DT8 3AE (0308 862814)

Broadwindsor

The White Lion, The Square, Broadwindsor, Beaminster DT8 3QD (0308 68855)

Marshwood

Mrs Ann Studley, Marshlea Farm, Marshwood, Bridport DT6 5QD (0297 7370)
Mrs T. Robinson, Long Acre, Marshwood, Bridport DT6 5QJ (0297 7207)

From Thorncombe

Mr & Mrs J. Jeffery, Bere Farm, Winsham, Chard, Somerset TA20 4JQ (0460 30207)

Penn

Mrs M. Chapman, Penn Farm, Charmouth DT6 6BZ (0297 60428)
Mrs Chapman (junior), Pennwood House, Penn Farm, Charmouth (0297 60724)

Lyme Regis

New Haven Hotel, 1 Pound Street Dt7 3HZ (0297 442499)
B.C. Harding, Coverdale Guest House, Woodland Road DT7 3AB (0297 442882)
Mr & Mrs K. Longley, "Petit Bot", Hill Road, DT7 3PE (0297 442674)
Mrs T. Franklin, Norman House, 29 Coombe Street DT7 3PP (0297 443191)

FOLLOW THE COUNTRY CODE

Enjoy the countryside and respect its life and work.

Leave livestock, crops and machinery alone.

Guard against all risk of fire.

Take your litter home.

Fasten all gates.

Help to keep all water clean.

Keep your dogs under close control.

Protect wildlife, plants and trees.

Keep to public paths across farmland.

Take special care on country roads.

Use gates and stiles to cross fences, hedges and walls.

Make no unnecessary noise.

To enjoy the best of the countryside

Join The Ramblers.

Explore the many hundreds of thousands of miles of Britain's beautiful footpaths and receive our exclusive Yearbook full of information on walking and places to stay.

Plus regular colour magazines and newsletters — free of charge.

You will also be entitled to valuable discounts at outdoor equipment shops.

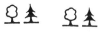

And at the same time you will be helping us to protect the countryside and to look after Britain's footpaths.

For further information and an application form, drop a line to:
The Ramblers' Association, 1-5 Wandsworth Road, London SW8 2XX
Tel: 071-582 6878